best new poets
2009

KIM ADDONIZIO, EDITOR

Jeb Livingood, Series Editor

This book was published by Samovar Press LLC, Charlottesville, Virginia,
in cooperation with *Meridian,* www.readmeridian.org. For additional information
on *Best New Poets,* see our Web site at www.bestnewpoets.org.

Cover photograph by Kevin Russ

Text set in Adobe Garamond Pro

Printed by Bailey Printing, Charlottesville, Virginia

ISBN 13: 978-0-9766296-4-1

ISSN 1554-7019

Contents

Introduction

Welcome to *Best New Poets 2009*, our fifth installment of fifty poems from emerging writers. In these pages, the term "emerging writer" has a narrow definition: here, it means someone who has yet to publish a book-length collection of poetry. Like the rules for many anthologies, that one is, perhaps, arbitrary. But the main goal of *Best New Poets* is to provide special encouragement and recognition to new poets, the many writing programs they attend, and the magazines that publish their work. And, of course, to deliver an accessible, eclectic sampling of emerging poets to you, the reader.

From April to June of 2009, *Best New Poets* accepted nominations from each of the above sources. For a small reading fee, writers could upload two poems as part of our Open Competition. A month earlier, writing programs from around the United States and Canada had sent free nominations of up to two writers, whom *Best New Poets* later solicited for work. And the anthology also asked literary magazines across North America to send two of their best recent poems by writers who met our definition of "emerging." We asked that the poems submitted either be unpublished or published after April 15, 2008. So, not only do new writers appear in this anthology, but you're also seeing some of their latest work.

In all, we received over 1,800 submissions, most of them containing two poems, for a total of roughly 3,500 individual poems. Seven dedicated readers blindly ranked these submissions, sending 175 manuscripts to this year's guest editor, Kim Addonizio, who selected the final fifty. Those seven readers—Evan Beaty, George David Clark, Jazzy Danziger, Laura Eve Engel, Julia Hansen, Lilah Hegnauer, and Terence Huber—deserve special thanks. All are practicing poets, and like prior readers, they worked hard to include not only poems they liked, but also those that they thought might interest someone with different tastes. Laura Eve Engel warrants double thanks: she came back as a reader even after I inadvertently left her name out of last year's introduction.

Best New Poets has always been an organic process—changing from year to year—and I think that is part of why it has survived and grown in a turbulent publishing industry. I tried to pitch the book to publishers as early as 2002, and, no surprise, got polite but firm rejection letters in response. Poetry books almost never make any money, poetry anthologies especially, and the publishers' hesitation to take on something like *Best New Poets* is understandable. Year after year, we hear more gloomy reports about bookstores closing, about yet another major house gobbled up in a corporate takeover. It can become depressing. The days of an editor like Saxe Commins—someone who took young writers under wing, often working with them for the totality of their careers—appear gone. Oh, the big houses still take chances on a few new voices, and they certainly mass produce the brightest literary stars, but that vast middle ground is suffering in drought.

Yet, while traditional publishers are struggling, small presses can reach more people, at lower cost, than ever before. Desktop publishing software has allowed anyone with a computer and an eye for design to produce a professional manuscript. Print-on-demand can create almost instant publication, and more traditional offset printing gets cheaper by the day. And there are even bigger changes looming—digital distribution through devices like the Kindle, the Palm Pre, the iPhone, and who knows what technology is just around the corner.

For the time being, *Best New Poets* is stubbornly clinging to a quality paperback produced by offset lithography. There is just something wonderful about holding a book in your hands, about giving poetry some room to breathe on the page. I have sometimes joked with students that I'll start publishing on a Kindle when I see them lugging Kindles to class. But then I got off a university bus a few months ago, and a student was sitting under a shady tree reading a Kindle version of the *New York Times*. Meanwhile, many new graduate students at the Darden School of Business at the University of Virginia have received free Kindles as part of a pilot project. So maybe we're headed that way. Digital distribution has certainly shaken the music industry to its core, and with the paucity of bookstores in most towns, text may not be far behind.

Today's consumers demand instant access and delivery. Just as record stores have almost completely disappeared, the day of the brick-and-mortar bookstore may soon end, and we will all be worse for it. Even so, perhaps we shouldn't worry so much about *how* poetry reaches the reader, but that it reaches them at all. In the end, that is the goal of this book anyway—to highlight new work from new writers, and to push it out to a broader audience. Thanks to the University of Virginia Press's efforts to promote and distribute this anthology, we're reaching that audience. But the lion's share of credit goes back to the poets in this book and its earlier editions. Those poets live in a generation of Twitter and Facebook, amid all the hustle and din of the Internet, and yet they've chosen to slow down, to turn inward, to find beauty—and something true—in the written word. "Poetry is life distilled," Gwendolyn Brooks once wrote. Whatever the medium, it is reassuring to see this next generation of poets attempting the same frustrating and seemingly impossible distillation, when the general impulse is simply to click "Add to Cart" and move on.

—*Jeb Livingood*
University of Virginia

Amanda Chiado

Openings

Don't think about the ship inside the bottle. It really makes tenderness difficult. I would if I had a mouth. I would if I was not a buried roll of quarters. I wish I could forget my hoax of parts, gem of mouth. So they said ruby. One called me Ruby. I should have saved the black pearl from the fire that I started. I should have saved the photos of the bread rising, my lineage of paper dolls. I flip pages to find burnt words that are shaped like me—curved on the outside, but sharp in the middle.

Amanda Pritchard Moore

Las Altas

If you're asking did I fall asleep against the Mexican boy's shoulder, then
          the answer is yes:
we were the youngest passengers.
The gentle bucking of bus over patched potholes
and the warmth of him through his jacket were enough for me.
          We weren't in Oaxaca, nowhere
near the coast or city or country, just
some houses that seemed to go on for hours like a video loop.
Everything flat.
Everyone boarding the bus and finding me,
my skin glowing, my blond hair shiny.
          It wasn't the boy who touched my knee.
It was the boy who slapped hands away from me like flies.
He never touched me.

None of the houses we rode past were mine, though
a woman in one served me rice
and left my clothes clean and folded on a bed in a small room.
I slept there.
Sometimes I would turn on the T.V. or use the telephone.
          No one seemed to mind.

In the morning, my breakfast was laid,
a napkin on the lip of the juice glass to keep out bugs,
thick heel of bread slathered in butter.
Mostly they didn't see me, couldn't
see me, wouldn't.
            At night I floated through the house ghost-like
dragging my strange clothes on the floor.

If you're asking how did I know when to get off the bus, then
            the answer is I didn't really:
after the third market on the left, maybe one hour,
after the two-story brown house and then the white one with a black fence,
somewhere there I whistled and got down.
            People called after me.
The bus creaked away down the street.
I wandered block to block,
            found my way by finding first
the Coca-Cola stand boarded up,
the only backlit Madonna shrine,
the crooked graveyard and the squat preschool.
The house opened before me
like moth wings.
If you're asking did I always go inside to sleep, then
the answer is no, not always.

Michael J. Grabell

Definition of Terms

Maybe it's because my mother met my father through the kosher butcher,
kosher meaning conforming to stubbornness,
butcher meaning to walk through life with bloody hands,
& me, the bread of this affliction,
leavened with the yeast of insistent immigrant ancestors.

Maybe it's because the night before their wedding, the cracked fortune cookie
warned, "You are doomed to be happy in marriage,"
doomed meaning inevitable guilt,
happy meaning one who is blind to missed opportunity,
the zest of an orange slice eaten from the rind.

Maybe it's because my mother grew up in Weehawken, New Jersey,
land of Lincoln Tunnel & of Aaron Burr's duel,
wee from the Austro-Hungarian meaning trust no one,
hawken from the Lenni Lenape meaning to clear one's throat
before saying nothing important.

Maybe it's because my father had a weak will & a weaker liver,
always flirted with the waitress, "I'll take a Sloe Comfort-able Screw,"
sloe meaning that which is derived from the wild plum,

comfort meaning the satisfaction of longing,
the way the juice hides the hardness of vodka.

Whatever it is, you won't understand when I say our love is like a hammer & sickle.
You will look at me with the eyes of your Irish ancestors
while we grind each day into a protective touch of cheek at night.
You will scrub the foundation powder from your face
but will never get rid of the burden that falls in the lines of your skin.

—*Nominated by* The Southwest Review

Megan Moriarty

Reasons Why the Birthday Party Was Apocalyptic

It was raining inside the house, so we were forced to move the party outside,
       where it was also raining.

There were locusts and frogs and some other things.

We played Pin the Tail on the Reason My Life Feels So Insufficient, and nobody won.

Death showed up, and a rumor began circulating that he had spiked the punch.

All of the balloons left without saying goodbye.

Everyone agreed that the cake tasted ominous.

We broke open the piñata, and all we found was a smaller piñata.

Brandon Courtney

Memorandum for the Record: Evidence/Property Custody Receipt

End:
1) Chronological Record of Medical Care (SF600) ICO The Human Remains that are believed to be Petty Officer Third Class Benjamin A. Johnson, USN, 090-64-2820 of 23 Nov 01
2) The purpose of this memorandum for the record is to document the following facts regarding the subject human remains:
   a) Received custody from LT Mat Kerver, HC Detachment on or about 1630 on this date.
   b) The only personal effects were received are:
      i) Wallet containing
         1. Geneva Conventions Identification Card (DD Form 2)
         2. Department of the Navy Gemplus Identification Card
         3. Great Lakes Credit Union Check Card Visa
         4. Blockbuster Rewards Card
         5. AT&T Phone Card
         6. Cyber Zone Card
         7. AAA Card Plus RV in name of Stacie Haas
         8. Value+ Phone Card; $20.00
         9. Verizon Calling Card
         10. A believed-to-be-foreign note for 1000 Dinar

11. HSBC Card
12. Barnes & Noble Readers' Advantage Card
13. New York Driver's License

ii) Contents of Miscellaneous Written Notes: All notes are transcribed in original form

1. Note 1: Dreamt that a girl followed me from the subway on 169th to Briarwood until she realized I wasn't her brother. She had broken glass in her hair and started crying because she was lost.

2. Note 2: Dreamt last night that there was a lobby of young girls dressed in yellow at the Hotel Giraffe, resplendent light coming off the East River, I stood at the bar reading the Sunday paper.

3. Note 3: Dreamt of white dwarfs falling in Brooklyn Heights, of fireflies in mason jars, rusted silverware, warm milk, transistor radios, women's breath and kookaburras in Queens.

4. Note 4: Dreamt of the recent snows in Columbus Park, where I went from antique shop to antique shop looking for my Father's 1967 Underwood typewriter.

5. Note 5: Dreamt early this morning that traffic was stopped along the Williamsburg Bridge, I watched the pedestrian traffic throw dead sparrows into the East River.

6. Note 6: Best dream of New York since the deployment. I dreamt that I stopped and watched Oscar Peterson play in a bar between West 10th and Fifth, by NYU. After the performance Oscar and I went to a delicatessen on 12th and drank coffee where I burned the roof of my mouth.

7. Note 7: Dreamt of riding the Thunderbolt rollercoaster on Coney Island, although I was young when they tore it down, there were small fires in the wood framing, but the structure never fell. A man walking the beach offered to sell me a portrait of Stacie and me together, even though she wasn't there.

8.   Note 8: Dreamt of a black chalkboard in the basement of a church, a Sunday school room in Brooklyn with the word "Jesus" written in cursive.

iii) The personal effects listed on enclosure were not received.

1.   9 Millimeter Handgun

2.   Two Ammo Clips

iv) All miscellaneous notes have been hermetically sealed and shipped with remains.

Michael Verschelden

American Erasure

I   Darkness More Like Being Free

Call me Crazy Horse; ain't my name
but don't want no more trouble. I
done me five years & got twenty
years without parole, what they call
life. Yessuh, can see darkness more
democratic than light. Lynched this
man down in Waco & they burned
him. Sewed up his ashes in little
cloth. Sold 'em ashes to the people.
Then at the barrelhouse a white boy
got hisself killed. There was some
shootin' & they said I done it. Well I
dunno, birds got chained to the sky
& freedom makes fugitives of us all.

Went to the penitensha you know,
shaved my head clean as yer hand.
At Parchman, Lady Day learned me
the blues. It ain't too bad but it ain't
like being free, what they call
liberty. In my time, I been a ditch
digger. Work for the Wright brothers
diggin' sewers. They say I'm
too old to dig no more, but for why,
I'm used to doin' it. Ain't gone
flyin' close to no sun, all the fixin's
got to be fixed down here & ole Crazy
can fix it. Stick to a ditch, I say, poor
Atchison gal got swallowed by the sky.

II   Mascara in Smokestack

The skinny on tonight's fireside chat:
Bardot bikinis, bulimia & the Battle
of the Bulge. Hosiery on butterfly
legs, Lady Day listens by slit blinds,
the railroad line's lust for a wolf
whistle. The eraser smudges &
smears mascara in smokestack. De
Kooning snatches enameled smiles
from *LIFE* magazine. Smoke loses
itself in its lack of eternity, a locust
shell wind between beauty & rotting
redwoods. In the winter fashion
preview, Jackie O bleaches caked
blood from starched cotton.

Wool-flesh greases Willem's wrist-
swivel ferrule. Velocity dovetails
into sex. Limbs, torsos & faces
are crudely collaged, seizures
wrestled smooth. Marilyn
as landscape, her voice looks
like paw prints in lipstick. She
poses in *Playboy* pastels &
the flesh disappears. A garter
belt tries to flag a ride, but poor
girl you can't peek behind goose
bumps. Leotards without a leg,
stockings like empty silk, yellow
underwear still warm to the eye.

III   Tramp-Poor People's Campaign

Carp-bait ripples over barbed wire &
cotton gin fan in the town of Money.
Threshing-floor shadows swayback
a slowdrag tango over facing chairs.
All's misalliance. Yet why not say
what happened? As the founder of
the Tramp-Poor People's Campaign,
Charlie Chaplin refused a stunt
double. Balancing on the rim of his
bath, he slipped out the window into
the motel's clump of smoking brush.
You know the rest of the story. In
Laurel Canyon, Charles Manson is
surrounded by doves at sunrise.

Shotgun houses in silence, static
electricity of dust, exfoliation
of the flesh. Chicken-wire covers
a vertical patch of grass growing
on the wall. An underground-road.
Emmett Till whittles a rucksacked
raven with a sun-tanned scarecrow,
but poor boy you can't shed your
skin. Tarred newspaper clippings
hang in strips like black picket
fences. Rubber tires beached with
dirt & gasoline dreams, a magnolia
welded into blossom, petals
perpendicular like an open casket.

IV   "The Unaboober" Festers in Your Breast

On your stomach, my knees straddle
your hips. Your white blood cell
count stabilized three weeks too late
for treatment. Ashen flesh molds to
kneading knuckles. Malignant mulch
festers in your breast. I knob thumbs
into your lower back until you yield.
When I peel away, you dead in
dream, I am almost convinced the
hands can heal. Next chemo session,
your right hand squeezes into a fist
to attract blood. With every puncture
your left hand clutches mine &
you stay as silent as a godhead.

Yellow strips of insulation coil beside
stacked sheet rock. Drill bits half-buried
in the dust distinguish our living room.
Surveying the destruction, our neighbor
jokes my mother has become "the Unaboober."
Shedding gauze, my mother unveils a crater
concaving into her chest. Hair succumbs
in graying strands strewn like tinsel on
the black corian, clogging the drain.
Toenails turn a brittle yellow before
peeling off like the skin of a banana.
Through a port between muscle linings,
the chemo drips into her aorta. Atria
empty & the flesh resists resurrection.

V   Jaundice Hospice

Boxwood windows & pivots of pink
portable toilets surround Central
Park. Faces inside torsos, arms are
mistaken for legs, hips for breasts, &
fingers for thighs. Cylinder, sphere
& Roy Cohn are stitched into the
patchwork quilt, but AIDS won't
be the coroner's cause. Jaundice
flowered his face into forsythia.
Stuck in the subway turnstile,
Lady Day & I spy propaganda
penalty kisses for Julius & Ethel.
His frames fogged, smoke smolders
from her thrice-baked head.

Ambulances line up on Beale
St., ready to race for the bodies.
Hooverville's Cinderella is sweepin'
sidewalks & will vein a high-heeled
H.I.V. needle for a slice of pumpkin
pie. Hospice & home. Not known
from his face, but the gaiety of
his gloves, you can pay, poor girl,
to watch circus-side as Jack Johnson
flickers like four white Communion
skirts in the basement of the 16th St.
Baptist Church. Like hairspray in
spring sunlight, the Great White
Hope won't last a round in the ring.

VI   Stare of Stacked Caskets

My father was raised in the funeral
home of St. Marys. My grandfather's
marathon trophies lined the corridor
before a pinched neck vein absolved
his days & I discovered the closet
of stacked caskets. I climbed in with
action figures clutched in my hands.
Seizure, growl & quiver, the elderly
family golden retriever bared yellow
incisors. My mother said he had a
brain tumor like my father, whose
face was wrinkled like wet headlines.
In the backyard, coated in a fur
of dead grass, he barked at nothing.

My father hates being late for
God or someone else's schedule.
Sunday morning, the security
guard nods & punches #26.
Suitcase snaps open as I stare
through glass walls at downtown
streets. The people are so tiny I
rearrange their faces. I scratch at
my dim reflection because I can't
shake the notion that a spider's
web is caught across my face. When
he's gone for his daily appointments
with God, Mom points me to photos:
"That's how you stand, that's you."

VII   Stoplight Blinks Double Mastectomy

The perfect image of a priest from
Desolation Row, the Phantom of the
Opera gleams like a moonbeam
trapped in a gasoline stain. At KFC
for Thanksgiving & hunched like a
chain link fence after a flood, Lady
Day skins "Solitude" alive. Home to
go. The Phantom masticates on fried
double mastectomy & prays as if he
is all terror & hands. Chins genuflect
when a razor finds their throats.
Chicken bones inside the cashbox,
Lee Harvey waits by the fast-food
window, bus ticket in his pocket.

1963: the first-born, Bill, skips high
school for the seminary. Neither James
Dean nor old enough to strike matches
on his jeans like the Man with No
Name, my Uncle Jimmy walks like
a broken headlight, hiding behind
hedges when the doggies from Fort
Riley scream by. A stoplight blinks
yellow as he lies on the asphalt haunted
by approaching rubber. My grandfather,
a medic in the Bulge, knew soldiers
too stubborn to dodge the breeze. &
Uncle Bill never became a priest,
his pulpit replaced by a Phantom.

VIII The Chemo's Epicenter

I cannot keep the world outside my
eyes. A snapshot, lurid, rapid, garish,
grouped, heightened from life,
yet paralyzed by fact. Fragments
of my father are shorn around the
epicenter of his exposed cranium.
He's too self-conscious with barbers
to hassle hair the radiation spared.
My mother drapes a cream-colored
towel about his neck that stiffens
his posture as if he's sitting for
a portrait. Scars on his scalp deepen
when kitchen sink moons summon
shadow from kitchen sink flesh.

Running, friend, is my spiritual
cud. Rhythm-a-ning to gravity's
hook & graft, hollyhocks tilt
in their traffic of color. When a few
strands resisted the chemo's
onslaught, my mother adjusted
a dusted antique & laughed with
her reflection. She borrowed
my father's razor & donated
the wig to her nieces for dress-up.
Now with scissors in hand,
her hair has the hint of curls. & no,
friend, there is no such thing as
a small, local cemetery.

IX   Operation Sing Spoonfuls of Napalm

Spoonfuls of gold, spoonfuls of oil
spill over the gulf coast derrick.
Drained gangrene & Antietam Creek
re-imagine the fountain of youth.
Camouflaged flesh whiplashes in
the twilight leverage of a booby trap.
Oppenheimer's smoke clouds billow
into a chess master's brinkmanship.
Iron Curtains & the Wizard of Oz
sing spoonfuls of napalm make
the medicine go down, down, down.
Lady Day & I eavesdrop as Coltrane
dedicates packets of cocaine to
God: psalms of saliva & blue veins.

Uranium atoms & rosary beads,
Trinity on Palmetto Sunday.
Crows canvas the victory garden
Los Alamos for vanishing points.
At the bedside of Terri Schiavo,
Sleeping Beauty falls to her knees,
but poor girl you can't return
to your Starbucks-less tower.
A big stick diplomacy: Operation
Rolling Dominos piggybacks on
parables of apocryphal Tonkin
torpedoes. Behind chrysanthemum
curtains, the emperor's lotus
sutras oval twice over the divine.

X   The War Be Damned: A Three-Legged Blues

Monday nights at Minton's are for
cutting, percussive punching on the
black & white. Detroit flamedances
to pizzicato snipes from upright bass.
When you order tanks to trumpet
the National Guard like Diz, home
is twelve stops from a three-legged
barstool at the corner blind pig. Mid-
air bricks mime syncopated silence
through Bird's alto sax. Timbre
be damned, flatted fifths trench
Monk's staccato low in jelly roll
until angular accents align
symmetrical with Storyville.

Dressed in zoot suit, frayed tie &
platooned on 12th St., you spit
phlegm into buckets of blue paint.
Fingerprints remain on the triggers
like reluctant kisses, preemptive
strikes against your insurrection
blues. Lady Day moans raided
riffs, cross-stitched hems cursed to
the swing of a paddy wagon shadow.
The Great Society & the War
on Poverty, you can't sweat-smear
hocked harmonies as if you had
Paradise Valley stashed
in your back alley checkbook.

XI   Flesh My Flesh Will Absorb

What the hips assume the hands will
assume. Dead bodies never drown,
anonymous faces but a carpenter's
problem. Dumped over the rail,
its congealed limbs crash into Pea
Bridge Creek with the confidence
of a .38 slug desecrating a lung.
Water is as unreasonable as death.
A broken branch holds a head steady
for the sun's slant to confront.
Poor weatherman predicts humidity.
Decay deliberates in this Carolina
creek over John Doe dreams. Flesh
has a deeper memory than the mind.

Tongues know the allegiances of
water, the responsibility to thirst.
My palm pressed to the pool in the
ceramic sink, the surface grasps
my fingertips. Each ripple appeases
a pulse as water unwrinkles in unison,
unlike the flesh. The scalpel's search
for a seam is futile. The reservoir
cleaves within. When I tear the cold
rind, a gasp of pale smoke perfumes
the pink beneath my fingernails.
If a droplet spills onto my wrist,
my flesh will absorb your memory,
recycling with a residual grace.

XII "Vaudeville on the Levee"

Wet-on-wet strokes wash over
sandbag & sediment. Smoke rumors
& a freight engine strand us half-past
salvation on a voodoo-remedy. The
levee camp gambler rattles snake-
eyed dice in his dentures. Home in
a chicken-soup stadium dome.
Costumed as Knights of the White
Camellia, we halloween sainthood
on stomachs of coleslaw. A stolen
Ford in the ditch, Bonnie yearns into
a nude sky & the fossilized gravel
of constellations as one slaw'd-saint
slices off Clyde's ear for a souvenir.

New Orleans beggar who looks
like Buster Keaton in black face,
tin cup tied to his shirt, gestures:
socks will serve as parachutes &
the reeds along the river will be
the umbilical cords of children.
He whistles "Vaudeville on the Levee"
& asks the Lord above for mercy
save me if you please, but poor boy
you can't silence yourself. Across from
the Santa Fe tracks, Jack Ruby's
tongue muscles a conclave of ribs,
his jaw a rendezvous between flesh
& a mortared basilica of bone.

XIII D.C. Coca-Cola Classic Red Scare

From the four corners of the Mall,
vending machines pitch the D.C.
Coca-Cola Classic Red Scare. Secret
foreign policy formula: reduce taxes,
recycle death & reuse dictatorships.
Veteran McVeigh pins Lady Day's
hair with a white gardenia Built
Rosie the Riveter Tough. Cola &
claw hammer in fridge, he returns
with baskets of smallpox blankets.
Marching through the firehose-swept
streets, every MacArthur will have
his dog's day parade the way a 767
kisses a skyscraper in slow motion.

A compost of split, knuckle & curve,
Satchel instructs the infield to squat.
Salted with torque, his arm's got
a midnight rider & a four day
creeper with enough atomic balm
to cryogenically freeze the Splendid
Splinter. Buckner swears he checked
under his glove for that Curse of
the Bambino Weapon of Mass
Destruction. A government bailout
blew through your legs, poor boy, but
the eighty-six year "Gawk & Haw"
is a Jet-Red Hawk Nation
banner Mission Accomplished.

XIV Save Yerself Alzheimer's Comin'

Gonna go from house to house &
preach. Not the church, just read to
people. Be a reader. No, not doin' it
now. Got somebody readin' to me.
Sho' was full of devilment, runnin' a
nickel brothel errand like Lady Day
to hear the victrola. But the blues
ain't a'ginst God, no ma'am. I was
in Hannibal, Missouri, passin' these
store-front churches & it's right to
serve God, but goin' to church ain't
gonna save no one. The blues 'mind
a soul that you cain't save yerself
without some down-home grace.

A ninety years widder-woman, don't
know exactly when I was born,
but you can figger it. Some days
I hate white folks fiercer than
Sherman's barbecue from
Hotlanta to Savannah. Some days
'spite misself, wish I was one.
But I know I cain't erase misself.
Ain't fittin'. Used to sing in
minstrel shows under canvas, but I
just likes the Bible & want
to find out who is who. Like today,
Alzheimer's comin' on & I don't
think anybody know who is who.

—Nominated by Kansas State University

Joe Wilkins

Notes from the Journey Westward

We died in the wagon. We had been sick
      since Wyoming, since the skin
of things had begun to pock
      with sagebrush and knobs of rock,
like the wrecked face of that bare-
      knuckle man back in Cincinnati.

We said our little prayers. In our fever
      the angels came. They had no teeth.
Tongues thick as snakes, sky-wide
      mouths, lips cracked as ours—
in this dry place, we decided,
      even the seraphim must thirst.

We ate the meat they gave us
      and were hungry. We drank the milk
and were thirsty. We pissed where we lay
      and did not understand. Yet we asked
no questions. We knew the only answer
      was farther west.

And here is what they did: Above a dry valley,
      up under a sandstone ledge,
they shoveled us in. If it weren't for the blood,
      our snapped and lolling bones,
dust the wagon left settling on our lips,
      we might have had the look of lovers.

Once, we were given an orange. This was early,
      just across the Missouri, the grass
thick, green willows weeping along the creeks.
      We would still walk then, a minute
here or there, hand on a horse's muscled rump.
      And at the very hour of our death, again
we tasted it, how we ate it peel and all.

Jamison Crabtree

Lyric

Donst says how we capable or not. Who
want they foibles kept as dainty. Box all our flaw inaudible
and we play pretend. We they, we do

starts up they doubt engine, shovels coal
until we smile pitch. We knows but refuses

they recall of what all she takes.
Her bag, it howl.

We heartlorn from they truth. On they line
we screws they stub arm, they assembly head
and learn it cry cry cry. I yr cartographer loves but

I straight busted on legend,
so let they local monster explain. He known you

and who want be known, not like that? Let you
takes yr sandstone interest
in anything beside yr image. Like, we

going present you deaf. Hear this: no one wants be known for what
they is, but what they pretend. You worth half yr

heels, yr suit, yr. No,
less. Go mow yr hair right. Prune they jean cuff. Yr ankle
is impeccable.

This what we loves you for.

David Silverstein

Metamorphosis

1: the absorption by the earth's surface
of sheep noted for fine soft wool, or
a woman's upper body and a fish's tail
on which people sit for a ride

2: this hallucinatory thread or network
between a group of persons where by one
carries DNA to another as a template for
the processes by which a metabolic process
and the bones of a person or thing is made
to produce artistic work.

325

2 : absorption by a corporation of one or more others

me·rid·i·an \mə-'ri-dē-ən\ n [ME, fr. MF *meridien*, fr. *meridien* of noon, fr. L *meridianus*, fr. *meridies* noon, south, irreg. fr. *medius* mid + *dies* day] 1 : the highest point : CULMINATION 2 : any of the imaginary circles on the earth's surface passing through the north and south poles — **meridian** *adj*

me·ringue \mə-'raŋ\ n [F] : a baked dessert topping of stiffly beaten egg whites and powdered sugar

me·ri·no \mə-'rē-nō\ n, pl **-nos** [Sp] 1 : any of a breed of sheep noted for fine soft wool 2 : a fine soft fabric or yarn of wool or wool and cotton

¹mer·it \'mer-ət\ n 1 : laudable or blameworthy traits or actions 2 : a praiseworthy quality; *also* : character or conduct deserving reward or honor 3 *pl* : the intrinsic nature of a legal case; *also* : legal significance

²merit *vb* : EARN, DESERVE

mer·i·toc·ra·cy \mer-ə-'tä-krə-sē\ n, pl **-cies** : a system in which the talented are chosen and moved ahead based on their achievement; *also* : leadership by the talented

mer·i·to·ri·ous \mer-ə-'tōr-ē-əs\ *adj* : deserving honor or esteem — **mer·i·to·ri·ous·ly** *adv* — **mer·i·to·ri·ous·ness** *n*

mer·maid \'mər-ˌmād\ n : a legendary sea creature with a woman's upper body and a fish's tail

mer·man \-ˌman, -mən\ n : a legendary sea creature with a man's upper body and a fish's tail

mer·ri·ment \'mer-i-mənt\ n 1 : HILARITY 2 : FESTIVITY

mer·ry \'me-rē\ *adj* **mer·ri·er; -est** 1 : full of gaiety or high spirits 2 : marked by festivity 3 : BRISK (a ~ pace) *syn* blithe, jocund, jovial, jolly, mirthful — **mer·ri·ly** \'mer-ə-lē\ *adv*

merry-go-round \'mer-ē-gō-ˌraund\ n 1 : a circular revolving platform with benches and figures of animals on which people sit for a ride 2 : a busy round of activities

mer·ry·mak·ing \'mer-ē-ˌmā-kiŋ\ n 1 : jovial or festive activity 2 : a festive occasion — **mer·ry·mak·er** \-ˌmā-kər\ n

me·sa \'mā-sə\ n [Sp, lit., table, fr. L *mensa*] : a flat-topped hill with steep sides

mes·cal \me-'skal, mə-\ n 1 : a small cactus that is the source of a stimulant used esp. by Mexican Indians 2 : a usu. colorless liquor distilled from the leaves of an agave; *also* : this plant

mes·ca·line \'mes-kə-lən, -ˌlēn\ n : a hallucinatory alkaloid from the mescal cactus

mes·dames *pl of* MADAM *or of* MADAME *or of* MRS.

mes·de·moi·selles *pl of* MADEMOISELLE

¹mesh \'mesh\ n 1 : one of the openings between the threads or cords of a net; *also* : one of the similar spaces in a network 2 : the fabric of a net 3 : NETWORK 4 : working contact (as of the teeth of gears) (in ~) — **meshed** \'mesht\ *adj*

²mesh *vb* 1 : to catch in or as if in a mesh 2 : to be in or come into mesh : ENGAGE 3 : to fit together properly

mesh·work \'mesh-ˌwərk\ n : NETWORK

me·si·al \'mē-zē-əl, -sē-\ *adj* : of, relating to, or being the surface of a tooth that is closest to the middle of the front of the jaw

mes·mer·ise *Brit var of* MESMERIZE

mes·mer·ize \'mez-mə-ˌrīz\ *vb* **-ized; -iz·ing** : HYPNOTIZE — **mes·mer·ic** \mez-'mer-ik\ *adj* — **mes·mer·ism** \'mez-mə-ˌri-zəm\ n

Me·so·lith·ic \ˌme-zə-'li-thik\ *adj* : of, relating to, or being a transitional period of the Stone Age between the Paleolithic and the Neolithic periods

me·so·sphere \'me-zə-ˌsfir\ n : a layer of the atmosphere between the stratosphere and the thermosphere

Me·so·zo·ic \ˌme-zə-'zō-ik, ˌmē-\ *adj* : of, relating to, or being the era of geologic history between the Paleozoic and the Cenozoic and extending from about

245 million years ago to about 65 million years ago — **Mesozoic** n

mes·quite \mə-'skēt, me-\ n : any of several spiny leguminous trees and shrubs chiefly of the southwestern U.S. with sugar-rich pods important as fodder; *also* : mesquite wood used esp. in grilling food

¹mess \'mes\ n 1 : a quantity of food; *also* : enough food of a specified kind for a dish or meal (a ~ of beans) 2 : a group of persons who regularly eat together; *also* : a meal eaten by such a group 3 : a place where meals are regularly served to a group 4 : a confused, dirty, or offensive state — **messy** *adj*

²mess *vb* 1 : to supply with meals; *also* : to take meals with a mess 2 : to make dirty or untidy; *also* : BUNGLE 3 : INTERFERE, MEDDLE 4 : PUTTER, TRIFLE

mes·sage \'me-sij\ n : a communication sent by one person to another

mes·seigneurs *pl of* MONSEIGNEUR

mes·sen·ger \'me-sn-jər\ n : one who carries a message or does an errand

messenger RNA n : an RNA that carries the code for a particular protein from DNA in the nucleus to a ribosome in the cytoplasm and acts as a template for the formation of that protein

Mes·si·ah \mə-'sī-ə\ n 1 : the expected king and deliverer of the Jews 2 : Jesus 3 *not cap* : a professed or accepted leader of a cause — **mes·si·an·ic** \ˌme-sē-'a-nik\ *adj*

mes·sieurs *pl of* MONSIEUR

mess·mate \'mes-ˌmāt\ n : a member of a group who eat regularly together

Messrs. \'me-sərz\ *pl of* MR.

mes·ti·zo \me-'stē-zō\ n, pl **-zos** [Sp, fr. *mestizo* mixed, fr. LL *mixticius*, fr. L *mixtus*, pp. of *miscēre* to mix] : a person of mixed blood

¹met *past and past part of* MEET

²met *abbr* metropolitan

me·tab·o·lism \mə-'ta-bə-ˌli-zəm\ n : the processes by which the substance of plants and animals incidental to life is built up and broken down; *also* : the processes by which substance is handled in the body (~ of sugar) — **met·a·bol·ic** \ˌme-tə-'bä-lik\ *adj* — **me·tab·o·lize** \mə-'ta-bə-ˌlīz\ *vb*

me·tab·o·lite \-ˌlīt\ n 1 : a product of metabolism 2 : a substance essential to the metabolism of a particular organism or to a metabolic process

meta·car·pal \ˌme-tə-'kär-pəl\ n : any of usu. five more or less elongated bones of the part of the hand or forefoot between the wrist and the bones of the digits — **metacarpal** *adj*

meta·car·pus \-'kär-pəs\ n : the part of the hand or forefoot that contains the metacarpals

met·al \'met-əl\ n 1 : any of various opaque, fusible, ductile, and typically lustrous substances that are good conductors of electricity and heat 2 : METTLE; *also* : the material out of which a person or thing is made — **me·tal·lic** \mə-'ta-lik\ *adj*

met·al·lur·gy \'met-əl-ˌər-jē\ n : the science and technology of metals — **met·al·lur·gi·cal** \ˌmet-əl-'ər-ji-kəl\ *adj* — **met·al·lur·gist** \'met-əl-ˌər-jist\ n

met·al·ware \'met-əl-ˌwar\ n : metal utensils for household use

met·al·work \'met-əl-ˌwərk\ n : work and esp. artistic work made of metal — **met·al·work·er** \-ˌwər-kər\ n — **met·al·work·ing** n

meta·mor·phism \ˌme-tə-'mor-ˌfi-zəm\ n : a change in the structure of rock; *esp* : a change to a more compact and more highly crystalline form produced by pressure, heat, and water — **meta·mor·phic** \-'mor-fik\ *adj*

meta·mor·pho·sis \ˌme-tə-'mor-fə-səs\ n, pl **-pho·ses** \-ˌsēz\ 1 : a change of physical form, structure, or substance esp. by supernatural means; *also* : a striking alteration (as in appearance or character) 2 : a fundamental change in form and often habits of an an-

Trey Moody

Climate Reply

Weather as if to repeat. Weather to read a name.
As if to ask a question, weather to strip the mane,

to feed the cats, to sleep. Go inside, weather to weep, split the maw.

Plant the plants, weather to eat the dead, their roots as if to speak.

Weather to number the names, hold the sheets
over bodies, blind as blue.   Weather as if to flame.

Scrape the storm of its howl. Cellar as if to swarm, night as if to rot.

Ground warm with flesh, ears as if to watch. Cover the eyes
with weather, weigh them down with skin.

The dead's steady hum, weather as if to win.

—*Nominated by Texas State University*

Sally Dawidoff

Night Manager

An hour after graduation, I had an interview. "Just wash your privates," Dad said.

Night manager of a home for the developmentally disabled. (I never slept at night;

might as well get paid.) Irene, the one quitting, began my tour in the basement, where

six people slowly sorted laundry—a life skill, she called it. They'd be quiet, she said.

Accidents were rare. Was I OK with wiping? When I was eight, Dad showed

himself to me. (I had asked, so that was no one's fault but mine.) Sure, I told Irene.

"It's good to be different. I am me. / I'm unique. Wait and see!" She would have known

the verse but didn't join in. Twenty-five tops, a sturdy woman with a level gaze.

Notions of myself: Fun. Unfazed. I was girlish in public, forgiving in intercourse, a recluse

come 2:00 a.m., chain-smoking, writing things down, weeping on occasion for about a minute.

*

The interview included pizza with the residents. When Irene started chewing,

I picked up my fork, speared a mushroom, and turned to beam at Jackie ("I Am Me" T-shirt;

white residue in the corners of his mouth). "Do you like doing laundry, Jackie? I myself

am an ardent laundress. I pre-treat, I soak . . . " *Laundress*—showing off. A spitty "Yes."

Arbitrary evenings, Dad would call; I ironed while he talked at me. Privately, I dismissed

whatever he had to say as crazy even when he was lucid, even when he was merely weird.

I myself was free to be eccentric, "quirky," what have you. (I wanted no part of it.)

Jackie sucked cheese off his knife. "Excuse me, sir!" Irene hollered from the kitchen door.

"We eat pizza with our hands!" I hid my fork in my lap, staining my interview skirt.

The job was "not a good fit." Irene may have sensed a reluctance of which I wasn't aware

to take a washcloth to a grown man's genitals. More likely, she could tell

I was a mixed-up person, terrified of breaking down; who couldn't rest

as long as others were awake, lest they make demands on me—spray their words on me.

Still, I was counting on becoming Irene. I counted on it for many years until my father died and I stopped sleeping altogether. A doctor gave me pills;

I knocked myself out and awoke in the morning and got out the door, life skills.

We disentangled fact from fiction; in time, I developed a maternal instinct.

Barbara Duffey

Thought Makes Everything Fit for Use

I.

I'm calling to ask
if I may be of
any use to you?

II. *Oxford English Dictionary*

16 e. *Forging*

III.

Before they knew her,
my parents' old dog
had been pregnant by
her own father when
she was spayed, and so
lost her puppies. When
she found a baby
rabbit in the yard
she held it between

her paws even after
it had died of fear.

IV. Ibid.

1820 SHELLEY *Let to Maria Gisborne* 222 Alas! it is no use to say, "I'm poor!"

V.

Possum, mouse, and cow
genomes, fully mapped,
hold clues for human
DNA, how to
make milk, how to chew,
what bacteria
to welcome to guts.

VI. Ibid.

10b. To have sexual intercourse with.

VII.

When my now-husband
first came to see me
he brought mum stalks—his
cats ate all the blooms.

VIII. Ibid.

11†b. To partake of (the sacrament); to take or receive (the eucharist).

IX.

I looked to see what
you held in your cupped
palm—it was nothing.

X. Ibid.

5†b. To have experience, or be engaged, in (war)

XII.

My mother asked me
to enter her in
the contest that picks
the best motherly
advice—the winner
and her daughter get
a trip to New York.

XIII. Ibid.

13b. To dispose or 'make an end of' (a person)

XIV.

Builders at the school
found a message in
pencil in a bottle
in the concrete wall,
signed with 18 names.

XV. Ibid.

1588 KYD Househ. Phil. Wks. (1901) 266 One should go helpe another as wee
see by vse in our own bodies; when the one leg is weary we can rest it on another
[etc].

—*Nominated by the University of Utah*

Roger Reeves

Kletic of Walt Whitman, the Wound Dresser

Here, the severed palms hidden beneath the improvised altar

of a priest, his black robe here, a wound,

here, feet here, legs carried back from a field

propped against a one-horse wagon here, barrel staves mark

fresh graves here, a peeled orange here, the boy

gone, here attend here God, these men, limb-less

the un-slaked those calling for a touch, this hand,

this thigh this bare chest, this blood-box,

this union, reed to blesséd reed I give my tongue

to any man's altar a single, scarlet lash flimsy, un-tethered, wanting,

let me hold and in my holding lose,

this sea of   *sons*   *I have sixteen, you have*

but one   *already lost,*   *touch*

these men   *in the silences*   *of their bodies*

if you cannot   *I will,*   *in every room,*

I will   *pour myself,*   *when they stutter or plead,*

gasp   *'lord, lord'*   *I will say,*

"here am I,   *enough,*   *open and be opened."*

—Nominated by University of Texas

Caitlin Dube

Self Portrait as Corpse

You who warped me, who sows me into sod,
you don't know what I do with the body,
it would surprise you, rabbit foot, lucky
shoe of salt, you who shod me, you who god
me. You who harvest the yellow rapeseed
pleas, in this field, I never make a sound,
you who ground me, who forgot me under
gold. You foretold this while you cut my throat.

The vessels cowered, then glowed. You who knows.
You who slows the hours while I grow sand
here, you who hacked me, tree, then axed me, you
who hovers. You who keeps me. I sleep, but
cannot take a lover. You who bind me,
tissues, marrow, you who slit the narrow
lung. I cannot breathe. You who ate my tongue.

I wheeze and make sounds of hunger, of field
I am Persephoneed under, longer
months than summer, longer weather reaps me,
you who would not spare me. I am seed which

spring wind never carries, the wind that scares
me. Tucked and shallow, as I imagine
breeze, the callow engine of forever

spins, but never does me in. You who wrought
this, you who brought me wins another pair
of limbs and skin, of mushroom hair. I root
where earth begins to end itself and sink
to core, it's hot. There is no air, there is no
plot, just one vertiginous layer and
spotted stones I'd leave behind me, and you

who gathers them, and won't untie me, won't
deny me the rock, the twisted vision
that calcifies me, a wintered bastion *Place*
of meaningless words, time and harvest, field
and bud. The body is done for, knotted
with rot, you who corpsed me, and buried me
and swallowed me and freed me from it.

—Nominated by Columbia University School of the Arts

Jules Gibbs

Pronghorn

The heart surgeon loves to carve the heart
of an antelope when it's fresh
and before the blood begins to clot
because it's so close to a human
heart—loves to show off his art
        furrow the blade precisely.

Oh, that passive, throbbing muscle
severed and still throbbing
passively, in his palm.
Such a big heart, such an old heart.

Extraction is exacting business. As is dissection.
He pulls a scalpel from his shirt pocket,
and it catches the flat light and he appears,
like his instrument, dainty and slight,
crouching there with men
and their weapons. Feminine.

The Wyoming grasslands fade
to the theater of foreground,

the plot, a man and his paramour—
a fugitive heart with four chambers
valves and septum, inferior vena cava,
      the atriums he names, the rooms within rooms.

It's nothing, death, just an object
in the crosshairs, setting the parallax
sighting the viscera, aiming for the pith,
      that bloody metaphor.

Mansion heart. Verdant heart. Grass-fed
Artiodactyl heart. Primitive, twelve-million-year-old heart.
Brotherly heart. Heart of concurrent evolution.
Landlocked heart. Humming, human, ruminant
involuntary heart.

Benjamin Dombroski

Elegy for the Emptied Prairie

—Gascoyne, North Dakota

The same flies that cloud huge, open eyes
   of dying bison beat thin bodies

against the windows of an abandoned
   one room school-house buckled to a wave

of tawny prairie grass. Slant of autumn
   light, wind thumbing through

open drill-books and pinned to a wall,
   the map of the world after the last war

yellows in the sun. Hawaii
   and Alaska await statehood.

English steamers drift at anchor
   off Cape Town and Calcutta. Sailors

sweating in heat. Their pink skin burns.
      And six petty German thieves dressed

in the drab of infantry
      are made to kneel in dew-wet leaves

deep in a wood along the Polish border.
      The very end of August

1939—quiet night, dust
      of stars scrawled through

interstices of ancient trees.
      Only the last one will try to run for it

and have to be shot in the back,
      dragged back to the ditch they had made him dig,

spit on, and shot again
      because the SS man who chased him

breaks his ankle in a shallow gulch.
      Country cleaved

already in the minds of Hitler
      and Stalin. Sweep of amber and endless

holy sky—wind the only promise
      kept across this emptied prairie we stabbed

roads and railroads through, dressed in language
      of dreams. The schoolhouse roof sags,

small, slate chairs are stacked in corners
      of the room, as if someone will come in early

to clean the floors and wash the last lesson
      from the blackboard—an exercise

in handwriting
      written in such florid script:

the quick brown fox jumps over the lazy dog.

—Nominated by Virginia Commonwealth University

Laura Davenport

Why We Don't Write about Kudzu

As if it's not enough that the 12:15
with its mile of coal cars comes to rest
fifty yards from the porch, idling awhile
before resuming a slow, northward shuffle,

or that the halting clank of car meeting car
echoes through sleep, line snaking back
along the lip of the river like a slow tune
you've crossed, re-crossed in dreams.

Or that the lights on the refinery blink slow,
powder the room red, the headlights of near-distant cars
on the county line cut through trees
like the sign of the brakeman's ghost,

still checking the rails. High schoolers parked
in the nearby field wait out his hovering lamp
as it glides close enough to touch.
And if the night is warm and wet,

salamanders will cross the dark, slick roadways
through the woods, seeking still pools
in the ditches. The lone heron at dawn
stands loose and alert in the shallows

beneath a bridge, a spark of aluminum
in the reeds. Still new to this place,
you will try to give meaning to these
visitations—As if a pine's particular notches

could be read. As if the sudden shift
of sparrows in flight could be a blessing,
and blessing were the same as touch. You can't know,
because you haven't been taught

how to name what overtakes you here:
At the iron works, closed since '73,
you could pose atop a hill of slag, imaginary
shovel in hand, read all the markers and still,

as you cross the dusty yard or climb
the boiler you would feel on your back,
like the weight of a hand, a target,
the ghost of this place, proof of rust

flaking off in your palms. An old dog
licking the shine on a potato chip bag
will remind you of the story of that boy
falling into the furnace—all those men

retreating, the hot ore emptied out
on the ground. How the next day they were turned away
at the gate. And some of those men who sit in silence
this morning on the bank, watching their lines,

and raise an eye to follow you past,
lazy, afloat, pale skin on the sides of your bikini—
they will hate you—your bare skin
reddening in the light. Still,

you will feel chosen, as if the river
curls around your body regardless, presses
you forward, and at your passing the woods
begin to unfurl heavy, delicate blossoms:

pink lady's slippers
and tough stalks of jack-in-the-pulpit
gleaming white through the undergrowth,
a telephone pole enmeshed: great vines

reaching up to the wires, stroking the river's bank—
that caress meant only to entice and punish,
cover and swell. To grow and grow.

—Nominated by Virginia Commonwealth University

Kelly Davio

The Way I Remember,

it was my older sister who walked barefoot
on the balance beam of a creosote-soaked
railroad tie abandoned in a field, and speared

the soft flesh between her toes. With tar stuck
at her heels, never looking down, she'd kicked
a rogue sliver pulled clear of the sleeper tie

and buried a fragment of oak in her skin.
She hid the wound from our mother
with a loose shoe, knowing prohibitions come

with bodily records of wrongdoing. At night
she dug at her angry skin with a crochet hook,
the oak breaking to smaller flinders

as I held a flashlight toward her foot, my eyes
shielded with a flannel sleeve, my voice reciting
times tables to cover her hoarse breath.

But decades later, I find a scar on my own
right foot, between second and third toes.
The raised tissue like a rubber band broken,

snapped to a curl beneath my skin. The position
is an exact fit for a kick at a rail tie,
the rough mend suggesting a want of stitches,

suggesting coal grown into the sinews
after years of my forgetting. Looking hard,
I see the ragged edges have striated,

sprouted spindle leaves like the vagrant foxtails
growing in fields, fields where I remember only
watching in fear, never walking a balance.

—*Nominated by Northwest Institute of Literary Arts*

Katy Didden

String Theory: Pyramus & Thisbe

Scientists say the key is gravity—its arc of motion
extends beyond perception into a million cosmos

mirroring our own. If it would woo concurrency
through the scrim of our dimension, I'd shape the way

things weigh into a word, and send new worlds
a sign made from the undrawn lines of apples.

Just thinking of simultaneity, amplified to the nth degree,
totally floors me. It is like knowing the pyramids exist,

though I have never seen them, their shadow sides wearing smooth
under the sole of the millionth stealthy foot,

while climbers scaling melting glaciers free another cold jade inch
for fish, and high on Mauna Loa tourists print the tread of rubber tires

onto fresh-cooled ash as they wheel oceanwards down Earth's
volcanic spine, and how all this is happening while I'm asleep in DC,

and somewhere else, out of reach, you're turning in the night
towards your wife. If I could tap the wall of all for points permeable,

I'd set my ear against a seam and cull clues of alt-you,
alt-I. What's the shape of the world where we are happy?

A place where it's still not strange for me to rest
against the length of you, say on the dunes of a slow-

paced oasis in the mirror of whose water moves the sky,
where cloud or birds the winking of an eye, and where

the wave-work of mirage blurs the shape of children
racing figure-eights around the palms. In the beauty of their bodies

you can see the trace resemblance of Thisbe, who, in the plot's alt-tale,
never feared the blood-jawed lion, already fed,

but waited clear-eyed, clean-veiled, until the lion left,
and in real fields beyond the wall met Pyramus

at the tomb of Ninus, under the moonlit branches
of the white mulberry, where he sat brewing tea,

munching an apple—food of certainty, symbol for
the harmony of all dimensions layered skin to skin,

of how all things begin, and how, fearless of falling,
one who left Paradise

wriggles in again.

Tana Jean Welch

Sometimes, the Trip Across the Continent Is Enough

—for Deborah Digges, 1950–2009

A white dress waving in the wind—
    not a distress signal, something stronger—
      is what I see when I picture you

            floating

  among the empty seats of the university stadium.

Bare feet, long hair, dress all eyelets and gauze,
    lacking the restriction of buckles and buttons,

            balancing

the height against the wind—
the student section, the press box, the nose bleeds.

A Botticelli gown
            waving to the lacrosse players
                        practicing their pitch below. Not a distress signal,

something stronger: the full sail of the best pirate ship,
                                    Queen Anne's Revenge.

*

Because channeling your troubles into poetry
                                    can only get you so far—

just like Lewis and Clark had to sometimes carry
            their boat through patches of prickly pear—

            the serious soul should never be landlocked.

Never have to carry the burden of three years'
            writing in a trunk on a pack-horse—the British
lurking behind every tree, Jefferson waiting
                        for his manuscript.

Sometimes, the trip across the continent is enough.
Six books, three husbands, enough.

*

Heading back east, Lewis twice tried
                    to kill himself,
either by gunshot or jumping overboard.
             What if Lewis had stayed on the Oregon coast?

What if all poets lived seaside, beach-ready,
                      watching
the waves pull everything out past the lobster traps, the ship-men,
out and beyond the seam.

*

The plovers eat grubs and run the foam line.
                    Pour warm sand
over your legs
and the earth quiets.
             Settled.

You no longer want to cut your hair short with a butcher knife
or color your naked body with Sharpie markers
                  and profanity.

*

Two-hundred-years ago
                    Mrs. Grinder, the keeper
of Grinder's Inn outside Nashville, found Lewis
                              with a razor,
cutting his flesh from head to toe. Bleeding
          from two bullet holes in his breast.
                              She slept
every night after, knowing his marred body
          was buried a few yards from her porch.

*

But the mother of the lacrosse player who found your body
          outside the stadium
                              is angry with you
for showing her daughter
the elasticity of the human form,
                              that the body

is just a body—warm liquid, wires and mesh, winters
of bone
          shining in the afternoon sun.

Everything else whipped
                    from the hem
of your waving white dress   to catch
          the most appropriate jet stream headed west.

Everything else flew over the Cold Spring Orchard, the apples
of Amherst—I'll tell the girl's mother

                                        you were half way
                                        across the continent
before you even hit the ground.

Gretchen Steele Pratt

Road Rising Into Deep Grass

All I know about barns I know
From the highway. They apple
The horizon with their fragrant
Rotting. Yesterday, I was in love
So the barns disheveled themselves

With frost and fat animals sleeping
In the sun. And somewhere, in back
Of the decades, my mother strings up
Tobacco leaves to dry in a barn north
Of Hartford. It was always August

And she worked under silky white nets.
All I know about barns I know from
The highway and I mean barns, not
Greenhouses, heaven's music boxes
Covered in snow and glowing—Just

The memory of red barns, of this wooden
World, soft-soaking in the long wet grass.
Somewhere behind the last century thunder

Washes over Glastonbury and my mother
Swings down silent from Aunt Pauline's

Hayloft, lands in a pile of hay and stays there,
Listening to it tick beneath her. At night,
The barns were swinging, slamming
Giants full of wind and pitchforks beside
Her tight new farmhouse. All I know

From the highway is that barns collapse
Plank by plank into the sky. I don't
Even know why they were always red.
Often I imagine them slowly moving
Toward each other, like islands.

Johnathon Williams

Dirge

Briars and weeds, garbage from the road,
but no shade to trundle through
where this pitted hill sinks the barrow's wheel
and we clutch the corpse to still its fall.
A dead dog. A dead Goddamn dog—ninety pounds
of German Sheppard, awkward as a bag of bricks
and stinking like a ditch filled with milkweed.
I push. My brother balances. We lean over the body.
We see-saw up the hill. A still day,
uncommonly hot, and school a month away.

Our house below the hill, its windowed face
a gaze of sun, mocks our glances, hides
its insides behind the glare. We want to know
if he's watching, our father, if he's pulled
the IV out again, sitting shirtless,
cheek to glass, warm in the light.
(We want to know if we're doing this right.)
We wrapped the dog in garbage bags—nothing else
would fit. A paw peeks out, pale and pink,
and my brother asks again how it died.

*

It ran in front of the car, okay? Two a.m.,
a dirt road, weak headlights, and I was tired,
driving too fast when I felt the bump,
the tire rolling like a baker's pin. I found the dog
in the woodpile. Sawdust filled its mouth.
I say none of this. Soon, we will take our shovels,
boot their blades till groundwater sogs, scrape
clay with our hands. Tonight, the coyotes will call,
and I will try not to think about that hole, how we stood
shoulder deep, looked homeward, and did not speak.

—*Nominated by University of Arkansas*

Brian Leary

The Trouble with the Mind

is that it only defects
once, & having done so, can never

convincingly reenlist. This is why

he walks the lines of his army & checks
his soldiers for beards. He says

Repetition is a way to get by in this world—

A lazy man embattled & years from home
may ride wild—hirsute & bareback—every

cantilevered bone bucking out of form:

the safe & sane continuity of it all
gone AWOL. He says

A beard is a handhold for enemy combatants—

One good tug pulls your face downward:
you'll be canting past your balance,

then breached, then bloodied, then turtled.

I'm asking what binds
knot body & mind. What ship's ballast

sallies forward into unseen winds

& does not keel. This fine line
where open air rides the ends of a thing—

a body a true thing—I'm asking you

does it hold unmoved to its every edge,
despite the boredom of everyday life.

Skin weathers terribly. This is why

he relishes routine—if all the brain's
chemicals fall into line . . . But Good

Soldiers, you make me nervous.

Chris Perkowski

What Nobody Thinks of When They Think of Time Travel

Let's say you pull it off.
I can't say precisely how; maybe
it happens like a movie:
A suit catches your eye
in some thrift store window,
musty air and razor-fine jingle
of bells mounted to the door,
and the cut of the jacket
feels right, even if the pants
fall a bit short. But it's enough
that you feel the part, you believe,
eyes closed on a rented bed, and
poof. Or maybe you're raking leaves
into piles, scooping damp armfuls
close to your chest, filling your lungs
with the earthy, silent scent,
and a falling branch puts you out.
The how is a distraction, a matter
of matter, crumpled gravity, things
you weren't built to comprehend.
Point is, you're then. Problem is,

you forget yourself: You never
stood at the center of anything.
The planet loops around, spinning
on its axis, not to mention
the ever-expanding rest of it, us
along for the ride. And there you'll be,
freezing your balls off, miming gasps
in the vacuum, while in the distance
sits a blue speck that holds
all you meant to set right,
the innumerable second chances
retreating for a second time.
Your young self lies unaware
in a backyard, beside a girl
whose name no one, not even you,
can bring to mind, but who is
indisputably and momentarily in love.
Trading guesses, a summer night.
Star. Airplane? Satellite.

Melissa Stein

Eight Questions

Quince

Squat and piggy, like the rest of him.
Barrel-body. Holding a hare by the ears
he tugs the skin off the meat,
relishing the *shhhh* of the fascia.
What's under the fur is a secret.
What's under the skin is divine.
Especially when brewed with port wine
and apple. Especially when roasted
with chestnut and quince. Do you ever
see yourself in the plush drain
of blood, in the marbled veins?
The figs are sweetest that have fallen
from the tree. The wasps with their jaws
bore holes in the slack meat.

*

Timepiece

The cool intelligence of branches
casting shadows on a forest floor.
Cog by cog, dismantling the time
to make it run, balancing the jeweler's
file to hone a weightless wheel's
fine teeth. Spotless white, the lab,
impeccable as a tulip's petal.
How do you breathe, knowing
that even breath will tremble
the branches? *Nothing is more delicate*
than this whir of tungsten
and copper. It nestles in my palm
like feather and bone. Its heartbeat
the only one I hone.

Gospel

His hands were thick, meaty,
callused, but so gentle,
as one might imagine Picasso's.
They were tearing out
the pages of a hymnal.
When he was done
he floated them, one by one,
over the balcony. In the village
below, heaven glided down
on wide white wings.

What do you believe in?
Blowing a globe
from a monocle of soap,
igniting the soul of a cinder.

Candles

Impossibly long and tapered—
white candles in a chandelier.
With them she tore the bread
to pieces, scattering crumbs
the ants would soon hurry toward.
The palace doors were open
to a breeze of spearmint and lemon.
When the soldiers marched
through the olive groves,
did they know they marched
toward cages? *If you pierce*
the breasts of thrushes,
string them together on red twine,
they still sing the sweetest tune.

Oil

Shell-sloped, pearl-smooth, combing
her youngest daughter's hair
without a comb, separating strands

that snag, arranging them along her back
in a dark fan. The courtyard is surrounded
by coconut and banana palms, fat
glossy leaves giving shade the way
goats give milk. Did your mother
kneel behind you this way
to smooth the ripe slick oil
in your hair? *I closed my eyes*
and breathed in the certainty
of love moving through
my own black hair.

Sparks, lights, and darkness

Two starfish brace against
the bathysphere's slopes
as it descends on its lifeline
of cable, swinging in currents
like a pendulum. *The red and the orange*
are as if they had never been,
and soon the yellow is swallowed up
in the green. And then the green
is gone. Two eyes spy through
fused quartz into the phosphorescent
gloom. What do you imagine
the universe to be? *Blue-blackness*
and sparks, then forever black,
the black pit-mouth of hell itself.

Arroyo

Cracked and leathery, curled
around reins worn smooth
with use, pulling left, then right.
And the familiar body beneath
obeys the silent intention.
In the bowl of the canyon
they pick their way through, surveying
dried creekbeds, deep fissures,
the blasted heartscape. After
cavalry devoured the land,
what sprouted in those miles
of conquering hoofprints?
When raindrops pelt the dust,
it's like a volley of gunfire.

Complexion

Faultlessly filed ovals, half-
moons rising without a hint
of cuticle, buffed to baby's-bottom
gleam: his fingertips lightly
grip the brush's tortoise stem,
fanning *Rose Flirtation* or
Blushing Bride high on the white
cheekbone, rimming the lips
in *Peach Desire*. These portraits
that you paint on human skin—

Each time I bring a face to life
with perfect care I fall
in love, and die a little
every time it's buried.

James Crews

Sex in the Rain

I imagined at first some kid & his girl had come
to this dank & rotting covered bridge searching
for a dry, hidden place to wait out a summer storm.
I thought they must have made love—I wanted
to call it *love*—& then had meant to memorialize it
with these words sprayed over the rest of the graffiti:
simply, *Sex in the Rain* in dripping, fading red paint.
But then I let my mind wander back to the dim-lit
caves of Lascaux, to the finger of the lone, ancient
hunter who traced those careful stick figures of stags
in blood & ochre. What if it wasn't magic or religion,
I thought, but raw hunger that drew what he ached for
but could not catch? Instead, I imagined a teenage boy
not unlike myself, skulking off in the middle
of an August night so humid he could almost taste
his own pulsing need with each new breath. See how
his flashlight beam coaxes a glint from crushed cans,
cigarette wrappers & shriveled condoms & watch
as he measures every letter of the most perfect
scene he's never dared to conjure: a man next to him,
their bodies one shadow as rain begins to tap a beat

on the walls of the bridge. He takes out his paint can,
shakes it & he writes it. He writes it big.

Rebecca Keith

Epistolary

Dear Drums,

Why can't you play yourselves? You're a whole kit
in a corner for godsakes, set up. Make yourself useful.
That boy isn't coming back, Snare, the song can't
live without you. Kick, that goes for you too. Toms,
we like the sound of you. You're a poor substitution
for the boy who could barely fit his knees behind you,
but you're the only sound that's something like him.

Dear Hot Lava,

I've found a place for you
in a kindergarten poem. You'll like it there.
They're fascinated with you. They imagine death
like you imagine it, an extreme sport. Say hi
to falling off Mount Everest for me.

*

Dear Keith Richards, et al.

Not the queen of the underground, despite
what you think. No more roses. When I'm in
the bathroom at the bar I'll think of you, come back
to finish my champagne, a pink cigarette
with gold filter. It will be okay to say cigarette,
because this is a rock song, not a poem. Let's face it,
you're getting older than that boy ever will.
No chance. Charlie Watts could fill in
when we record the songs that need drums.
That would be something, but no consolation.

Dear Mount Saint Helens,

One girl I know was born the day
you last blasted, the big time I mean
not the false alarm puffs a couple years ago.
Another girl I knew had to cover her mouth
with a mask for your ash coming down. She must
have been only five or so. You were just a bad dream
after that. I dreamt Mount Tabor
was as big as you, erupted down Hawthorne Boulevard,
and the higher ground I went for, across the river,
was a penthouse. My rich friend had moved conveniently.
Are you hot? Would you like a soda? Where are you going, and what
are you doing?

*

Dear Elizabeth Bishop,

Do you know ten strangers
share your house now? At least one of them
tries to channel you daily. We get daily
poems now over the internet if we choose to subscribe.
Who knew? That poem you wrote about Varick Street,
that's what Varick Street feels like. I imagine
translated into Portuguese it would still feel like that.
Steel feeling. Cast iron. It's a good street for taxis
when the Holland Tunnel's not backed up.

Heart,

Did you think
it would end up like this? A dog,
a house? Saving up
for a grand piano?

Dear Guy-at-Fanelli's-Who-Looks-Like-Mark-Twain-and-Einstein,

Are you really at the bar
every day? Did you think
it would end up like this? Do you
get ketchup in your mustard,
I mean, moustache?

*

Dear Anne of Green Gables,

How is Gilbert Blythe these days?
I hear Prince Edward Island
is heaven. It's that north sea
we fly over that looks so cold.
The way your hair was always
coming loose when you swept it up,
I would've pulled your braids too.

Earth to Love, Earth to Love:

I don't think that suitcase
is big enough. Do you read me?

Alex Dimitrov

White Fire

for Anne Carson

To describe how rain touches morning in Iceland—
where St. Christopher often leads travelers
in spring—is to cross the impossible
bridge between water to drink
and water that drowns.

If you're lonely enough, if you listen,
the wind will convince you, in its human-like
sadness—to open the windows
and let something in.

Watch as it lifts above the ice—
the unforgiving element—white
fire.

Remember, you too know something
about snow's passage to water:

how everything trembles when moving
from one form to another—how soon,
it is water that slicks your eye—
each lash burning
to put the fire out.

Chiara Di Lello

Center

gone turned off cut out the stars on the ends of their arms
women driven into hills

the viceroys' hair is the smoke of severed limbs,
they write treaties with the spill.

inland maps in the mud prints, weavers walking
stands of palms, lost bracelets

brute instrument breaks five point loom
star goes out // goes out

wind maps grow from their wails.

this is not a world that is coming
—salt, foam, fire—

spinning gone dark

the pipes in the palace burst.

they reach to pull their own hair, paint sea maps

gone dark the out the star // the star
bone shuttles heaped
the flow washes the street clean of streets,

with spinning gone dark

the kingdom flows out through the city wall,
from their feet comes current, underground creek

find the channel below the breakwater drawn in henna and spit

a road outside the village, the inside of their ears

women of the next world, hold out your hearts
and not your hands, not your hands

Adam Giannelli

What We Know

We live in a house on the edge of town.
Dust coats the floor and windows,
slumbers inside our clothes—
almost divine, the way
it gets into everything.
Our back porch looks out
onto wilting clouds and rows
of alfalfa, shade pushed
into the corners of the fields.
When it storms at night, lightning
disfigures the darkness.
We eat with spots on the silverware.
The plates are cold
and chipped from grief.
We lick them clean, feeling
the crevices with our tongues.
When the bread goes stale, we
give it to the children and they use it
to hammer nails into a board.
We walk with our shirts unbuttoned,
the rooms without curtains.

Our lungs flutter furtively
whenever we pass an open window.
Our scars slowly sink back
beneath our skin—
little, pursed lips holding their secrets.
Our tears, like our hair and nails,
have broken off from us
and stopped beating.
What we've learned about love
hangs in a narrow closet
beneath the stairs, wrapped
in tissue so it will not wrinkle.
What we've lost could
flood the basement
of every building in this valley.
Sometimes we burn our stories
page by page inside the oven.
Sometimes, we leave them
alongside the highway at night
to cry themselves thin.
Sometimes, we prop open
the front door, let the breeze reach
through the house, lie down
and tell them to each other
over and over.

—*Nominated by* Smartish Pace

Stephanie Rogers

On the Occasion of Her Annual Disappointment

I woke in the night and begonias flew from my mouth.
Happy Birthday: this could be a long one. You can imagine

the lump, fist-sized, throbbing in the throat from those
unraveling bulbs. Then, the girl who looks like me, talks

like me, lives straight and thoroughly out of laundry baskets
like me, she almost wept. Well, actually. I woke weird,

hand fat with sleep. The girl in my mirror shook, curled up
at the bottom, scratched the glass so hard a fingernail flew.

When I opened my mouth to calm her, *there there*,
the flowers gathered like ulcers, shot up from my stomach,

the long stem of the esophagus, then bloomed angrily
at the voice box. Begonias. And the girl who appears

in my mirror every birthday to carve her little celebration—
another year down and we're still here—screamed, delighted.

Okay, truthfully. I woke bleeding at the mouth, grinding
teeth. My tongue: stabbed by an incisor. Droplets bloomed

on the lower lip like the residue of wine. Sometimes,
I pour a bottle for the girl in me, when it's her birthday,

and no one has given her flowers.

Arnold Seong

Transplantation

Lugging peat into the garden
my father seemed, through the window
where I thumped on the piano, graceless
and strange under the humid crud, his shuffle
the humdrum plod of beginning a new
garden. Watching a moment, I changed,
then went to help my mother plant
sesame and *gosari*, crouching
the Asian way—feet flat,
ass to heels. My mother says
Korean cuisine was scavenged from
a scorched earth, an opulence
of weeds. Their lot, so filled with rocks
a shirtful of pebbles proliferated beside
each plant's divot, difficult fossils I carried away.
Everything, eventually, blossomed—
but that would take time.
I wanted it to be easier.
Instead I watched, at the end of each
heft and haul, my father's sinew
and eyes tighten, his cheeks flushed

and glossed with sweat; watched,
on each final pull, my father's
moon-round face, full
of anger with what he never had,
and what he couldn't give: what wouldn't.

Carolyn Creedon

Pied Beauty

Glory be to the guy who invented Missouri for money,
with its plateglass heat, its thick-tressed storms,
its power outages, its broken water mains;
glory be to these broken-up brick stoops full of women who sit
calicoed, bandannaed, laughing and fanning at their men
making finger v signs with light and dark roughened hands
who pull in from the Shop 'n Save and haul out silver bags of ice
from their Ford F-lines and pass them around;
glory be to Cedric's Fish Fry for cooking up everything
over a lit trash can before it all goes bad, glory to the beer
to be drunk while it's still cool, glory be to the E felony
of freeing the over-full hydrant, feeling the loose damp shirt
on the body; glory be to wearing nothing much, dancing with strangers,
glory be to somebody's six-pack of D batteries, for the flashlights,
for the boomboxes blaring the bleats of poetry, a band called pain,
glory to the little girl with her doll tucked football-style under her arm,
its boy hair crisped sleek in the middle, two like waves meeting each to each,
glory to her mommy, whose feet hurt, who's home now
whose love for this girl in this place makes her skin feel raw and soft;
glory for half a moon that haloes everybody the same this night
for the nest of debris and leaves we rest on, and later, in the hot dark,

while I wave a lazy magazine, glory to the found matches you touch
to our Jesus and Mary industrial candles, lighting up
your sweat-dabbed glorious face;
para que no me atormenten de nuevo sino que seamos salvajes en la gloria del espiritu santo.
Praise this.

—Nominated by the University of Virginia

Rae Gouirand

January

The last persimmon: a moon
a clear interference. A thing pressing

presses: the idea of a door
before the one who notices: moons,

branches. Gods of doors and
gates. Wind blurs: word. Braids dust.

Moons wait in all the waters
of the world. Numerous and definite:

I put my heart out to:
the light. It reads: itself not horizon.

Moon shining in still pool: eyes
casting: another center. What: you love

you cannot cup, lift out.
What you love must: be only what

you love: knowing what
goes unstirred: in the wind around.

Sally Rosen Kindred

Common Daisy

Take me petal, sepal, carpal.
Take me ache, thirsty eye:

be my surgeon. Be my scouring lamp.
With your dread sourwater dress

my wounds and the wounds of all
my springtime dead. I will

stuff you in sacks for the soldiers.
I will enter the tips of their spears,

enter blood sweetened
by breaking and receive

you there, astringent, stark
pouring-out of ash

stars. I want to fracture. Then
I want to wake:

your manic anthems shame
my sleep. Teach me

crack and flail, the bleached
dance of your crooked bones

chained around the day's eye.
Let the sun drive its tines

into our splayed hearts. Common
longing, send me home.

Pilar Gómez-Ibáñez

Losing Bedrock Farm

> *Think small.*
> —Richard Hugo

So I'm down to grass, belly down
where I spent the seventies, eyeball looming
over the tight-spun nest, the blades
shot green through dry roots. On my scalp,
the palm of heat. On the narrow
deer trail, gloss-black droppings.
Where the doe cut through the lashed tangle
of raspberry canes, a tuft of white
is caught, you might read like a signal
if you knew the language, like the flash
of my mother's hat where she gardens,
screened by the ancient wind-bent row
of apples. From here you can't see the house,
can't hear the silence in it. *No*
you say, *smaller*: in sun, the deer
pellets are glazed gold, flecked
with husk. The wind grazes me, floats
over the field. It touches the cedar,

lifts the green at the nape of its neck.
Such deep longing—*no,*
you say, *smaller, much smaller.*
So my mother weeding, kneeling
in the potato hills. She whistles. She works
the clump of mud free from roots,
tosses into the basket. Someday
she will leave him, it will take
twenty years, and all this
will be sold: thicket of thorns, orchard
past bearing, the deer's stamp in sand
south of the pond. What's possible
to sell. Land under her feet, field
under my belly, though by then I'll live
in the city, as if that's my home—*No,*
smaller, small, you urge—so here
in my pocket, a chunk of porcelain.
Some long-lost cup, white as milk.
Still glitters with dirt. Picked up
in the bean field, day before closing.
Woman who planted the apples. *No:*
her fingerprint. In the grit, a flake of mica
catches the light.

—*Nominated by* Indiana Review

Lauren Moseley

Summer

You told me two things while we walked through the gardens:
1. If you could be any animal, you would be a bear,
and 2. My hair was the color of a wilting magnolia.

It was the last day of good weather. At sunset, empty bottles
of beer and wine glinted everywhere. I banged a tambourine
till my fingers bled. You played guitar and we didn't argue.

I noticed cuts from the jingles in the morning, staring at my hands
while you cursed and threw pots and lids because you broke
a yolk in the pan. It rained all day—bullets of hail in the evening.

We bought tomatoes of every odd color that afternoon:
orange, yellow, green, purple. I was afraid to say I wanted red,
so we got the ones you chose and ate their mealy flesh.

Your moods made me want to shake you like an apple tree
and watch every memory we made fall to the earth. We didn't even
make it to autumn. Cicadas still buzzed fiercely for their mates.

Katie Schmid

Jobs

(*The one where you were a carpenter*)
Eight hours of the saw, electric,
and your hands dream
of the silver spin,
the cut,
pine and skin.

Everything you could make.
Everything that could unmake you.

(*The one in the Mitsubishi plant*)
You, made of tin,
thin as a violin string,
going where the fat
union man can't.

The belly of the smoke-
stacks. A length of time
unclocked. Black close
as cold fog. Imagine
the sudden arm
that finds you.

(*The one in the greenhouse*)
Repetition patterns
what's quilted on closed eyelids:
rows of posies,
rows of posies,
rows of posies.

Dirt ground
into furrowed hand.

(*The one where you hauled granite*)
A joke about Sisyphus: body
without self. Bowed
body strung bow-taut.

(*The one where you counted soybeans*)
Hill of beanscounter:

Everyone can amount
to something.

(*The one at the lumberyard*)
Storm spins out,
spiral widening the sky.

Hazard new hands given fork
lifts, hazard the levers, hazard
the hounding rain.

(*The one in the chemical plant*)
Into the drum
the turbine moves you:

Here, everyone knows someone
dead.

(*After hours*)
Eat an orange and
it's gone but for

the zest flesh
under the rind
of your nail,
the stinging smell,
the slow peel
going to seed.

Sara Elizabeth Johnson

How the World Was Made

In the ballroom light the filigree of our hand
bones entwined. And I saw the anatomy of your hand.
Anatomy of the book behind your face.
Anatomy of the sleeping eye, of the bleeding
star at the edge of implosion, of the mouth as it prays
against another mouth. Of the mouth remade
into the smallest island of finches. Anatomy of the sea
before the land fractured it. Anatomy
of the ancient ferns, the reptilian eye of the dark form
hovering between them. Anatomy of adagio,
of aria and the voice. Anatomy of the prayer between
mouths, of the space between words
in the book laid under the tongue. Anatomy of histories,
of each other universe entwining with this one—
a diagram of light and dark matter stretched
across the surface. Everything was veined. Everything
was given shape and bones and muscles to fill it.
Everything became mortal but I could hold it.
I could hold it, and it held me. I heard each thing stir awake.
I knew my faith made it so. And I knew the answer.

Take this mouth, these hands. This throat, its slender
tangle. It's all here. Take it all. Then breathe into it.

Andy Young

Cleopatra, Pregnant, Refuses to Let Marc Antony Leave the Bed Chamber

don't look to the east
                              where the sun rises,
watch it set with me in these ruddy shadows
                    arching over vaulted walls

lean back, daddy,
            my slave Iras will rub your soles
                              with sandalwood
Charmion help me spread the wealth
of our kingdom   before you:

slick wet banks of the Nile,
                    chambers where you sup
            and rest your crown

                    that's it. . . .
on my knees   your face floats above me
            as it did before my boat at Tarsus—

your nose straight as a Roman road
                    your Akhenaton lips made
                    for black Egyptian honey

what of the front, the swarming hordes?
          forget the Seleucids, the smoke-tinged air
          that tells us yes our providence is burning

I'll sing you still in nine tongues,
          lick your wounds   as I did in Tabriz

later we will test the poisons,
             eat the figs the asp slinks through

             now I am a pod of lotus seed
              splitting,

             inside me the next king stirs

knock back to the one knocking   twin my quickening

        listen with your hands to what we've made

Caitlin Doyle

Thirteen

There are as many years in you as witches in a coven,
devil's dozen, number of steps to the noose, no use
to rub a rabbit's foot or knock on wood,
you've had one too many birthdays than you should

twelve years they served Chedorlaomer   and the thirteenth they rebelled

   so you learned to read from the book your father
held before the fire but the thirteenth psalm proved him a liar
and in your heart you said the multiplication tables
must go higher   and then you began to bleed. Old dress filling with new need!

There were twelve branches in your father's book,
twelve kinds of precious stone; there were twelve loaves
and twelve bright springs   but now there's a month
no calendar brings   and now there's an hour no church-bell rings.
   There were twelve gates and twelve golden cups
and twelve fruits in the tree   twelve white pillars
and twelve tall sons   but now there's a gate where no boy swings.

There are as many years in you as petals on a black-eyed sue,
   seats at the last supper, spades in a deck; no sense to hang

a cross around your neck or throw salt over your shoulder.
    Your mother stiffens when you hold her.
Your mother pulls away and you remain on the steps
        of the school. She won't come again before the fall
    begins to turn; it may be too late then for all but snow and nests below the leaves
    and trees whose shaking is uncontrollable

give me back the child consolable
    taking your hand, may squeeze too hard
taking you home, may not say a word
but always audible   *give me back the child consolable*

    Always heard, your mother invisible
 as you turn and climb the steps or learn that an eclipse
 is the moon across the sun or discover that your age is divisible by none
or put your clothing on before the mirror.   Never nearer
    as you turn   or discern a face   ever clearer,

what is happening? An opening,   a breach, a loop of rope, a door? One step more,

the hands can't catch,   the hands can't reach,   the clock is wound   but
you're beyond.

—*Nominated by Boston University*

Joshua Robbins

The Man in Hopper's Office in a Small City

A kiss or rather the ruins of one: a swirl of dust

in sunlight, perhaps, as it mingles with the stifled love-cries
        of a hotel painting above an unmade bed

even after the lovers have left, checked out to wherever it is

        lovers go hours later driving a blue Chevrolet
down a two-lane highway in Kansas & watching a controlled

        burn's flames flutter, smoke braids rising

from black grass & becoming the ashen haze evening is,
        jotting down its regular inventory of empty silos & sagging

fence posts bound with rusted wire that mark the miles. But

        whatever it is, I'll never know it, trapped as I am
decades now, staring out spotless window glass forever at God

        knows what. Sleeves rolled & vest chest-tight, this sun-muted

office severe in its loneliness, I know you're thinking I could be
      your father years back, working late, distracted

by the thought of a woman not your mother, a woman who

      even now remains nameless, though it wasn't what you've
thought: Motel 6 & an hour for lunch, Jim Beam

      in a plastic cup, lipstick-smeared menthols, the alarm

buzzing get back to work, as if in your imagining of it you might
      find some shadowed truth made visible, something

like what would find you here if you searched long enough,

      something there in the foreground, maybe. Right there.
Something knowable, touchable, a single stroke.

Warren Heiti

From The Uncollected Works of Sallie Chisum

Billy shaved off his moustache
in my bathroom and now he's
smoking calm as a mollusc
his pearled vertebrae braced
against the snarled bark
of the vine   he breathes
serenely   bullets washed up
around his bare feet

And Garrett's resting on my bed
in his yellow raincoat
the oranges turning to cork
on the bookshelf and the sky
scoured pure as an oyster shell
with its purple whorl

After that we drifted I guess
I went west   Garrett
went to the red sands
in the east   Billy
went to the centre   lived
under a wrecked sky

*

Eclipse and the Pleiades hang
like a filigree earring
from the lobe of Ethiopia
and Garrett murmurs *the earth
is like a garden spider
in some large dark
house*

We're playing mancala at the table
he gathers his stones and sows
them across the board   seven
deer step across the dead cornfield

The web of the Milky Way stretched
taut as latticed steel across
the ceiling

He chews his wine-tipped cigar   his tin star
unpinned and hidden in his chest
pocket but I can hear it throbbing
like a pulsar in the dark

I place my fingertips on his wrist
but his pulse is a stopped watch
and the purple birthmark spills
into my lap   stains my skirt

A rotten orange   a toppled
wineglass   a spider climbing
the stars

*

I was rinsing cherry
tomatoes under the tap
when the angel fell
thru the porch roof
its arm a fleshless length
of star   the quills
of light razoring out
along the sixteen wings
and the wings within wings
and the atoms splintering
in the aluminum cranium

The voice loveless as the voice
of God   PROPHET   YOU
ARE CALLED   YOU
WILL BE BALD   YOUR
LIPS WILL BE CIRCUMCISED
WITH LIVE COAL   YOU
WILL INGEST A SCROLL INSCRIBED
WITH THE HOLY EQUATION   LOVE
= OBEDIENCE   YOU
WILL BE PURIFIED
BY FIRE!

Its scimitar arm
shone   its helicopter limbs
shone   its nuclear eyesockets
shone   its cerebrum
crunched another atom

It salivated battery acid
I noticed the neon corona
bolted to the atmosphere
around its skull   it held out
a blowtorch and offered to fix
my broken
soul

No
thanks I said but you
can fix that hole
in my porch roof

*

Sitting with Henry on the back porch
wearing one of John's white shirts
hot as noon at eight AM but quiet
tho Henry's hearing things I cant hear
I can tell cause his ears are twitching
I blow steam from the milk and tea
and still burn my mouth   pour a tumbler
full of ice and whisky   get up
go to the porch rail and lift the fallen
leaves from the wilted datura

There is a man whose mouth I sometimes
want   this tumbler of whisky better
than the first   it's harsher
hotter   days as hard as the glass
tumbler against the wood rail

A loose shirt and too many tumblers
of whisky   the man whose mouth
I sometimes want has left   he came close
enough so I could feel   so I could
feel   so I could hear   did he hear
he came close enough so I could hear
his heat   he came close enough   did he
hear   he came close enough   a loose
shirt   I heard his heat   too many
tumblers of whisky   and I want
his mouth   warmth was the first time
warmth was the first time   warmth was
the first time I felt   but who's counting

Warmth was warmth was warmth was
a man whose mouth I always wanted
and warmth was a man who is not warm
and warmth was what I remembered when I felt
the heat of his hand   when I felt
the heat of his hand thru my white
cotton shirt

Sitting with Henry on the back porch
wearing one of John's white shirts
smoking and lifting loose tobacco
and tea leaves from my lips and thinking
about you Billy   crows cool the sky
with their flight   but my shadow's
thin as my shirt and the sun
goes straight thru   whitens
my white shirt and turns
the wood of the rail
to wood

—*Nominated by* Event

Jennifer Molnar

Separation

Those who winter here bury
themselves in

earth as if practicing death
rituals

or else pass between trees, black-
eyed shadows,

dull skin rib-stretched, blank canvas
over bone.

All are not meant to survive:
early thaw

reveals a doe's dark carcass
sunken down

beneath the pond's thinning ice.
And still wild

crocus break through detritus,
bruised petals

splayed wide to catch distant light.

Danielle Cadena Deulen

Lovely

My sister accuses me of leaving
and staying gone. Her face has grown dim
as she waits for a reason. Musk and winter darkness
cling to the heavy curtains hanging
from her windows, crowding out the deep green
of camellia leaves, their thin tips scratching
the surface of her window, and beyond them
traffic blooming smoke in rain, thistle-weed
and wild grass growing in the busted
body of the pavement, no longer a smooth
gray bone the way it must have been
when it was laid down a decade ago.
"I don't know," is all I can say. I know
fog stands in the hills of the park down the street.
And on the other side of the park, a reservoir.
And on the other side of the reservoir an avenue
of warm light and chatter, scones and fried pork,
rain beading up on the surface of umbrellas, buses,
airplanes breaking through stratus to blue sky.
Above there are people nodding and smiling
through compact windows, looking down at rain clouds,

lightning, whole swaths of sky suddenly radiant
like pearls, like the meat of the apples we ate
in the summers of our childhood. *Translucents,*
they were called—tart and delicate, ripe with light.
That was so long ago, sister. All forms, from a distance,
are beautiful. We are tied to that beauty,
to those forms, until we die. And so we try to evade
the shapes others make of us, and the sense
of ourselves built on those shapes. I was not
the only one to leave. Remember those boxes
you kept beneath your bed, tied with pretty red ribbon?
Remember the night you slipped out through
the window, barefoot down the slant of the roof,
dropped like dark fruit into the streets alone,
left me to find your untied boxes,
each filled with the skeletons of birds?

Eric Weinstein

Diagnosis

i have an unhealthy attraction
to hospitals.

i come in and unbutton my shirt,
insist that something is wrong with me,

beat on the triage nurse's desk,
on the glass door to the trauma unit.

four hours later i am informed
there are pieces missing,

whole organs, removed like batteries,
and yet my blood still moves.

the doctors wash in and out.
lub-dub. lub-dub.

e pur. e pur.
(and yet. and yet.)

four days later, at my kitchen table
the phone rings.

good news, they say. you're missing
just four chambers of your heart,

four base pairs in your dna
(adenine, thymine, cytosine, guanine),

at most four fingers from each hand.
—oh yes, the facts are in

and you can live without your heart.
(we have machines for that.)

Keith Leonard

A Brief History of Patience

A hundred or so lobster pots cut loose

and chock full of dead catch. Broken jaw

of a pier. Summers I learned

there were four ways for a wind to blow,

one shepherd for a rising sea.

What once was buried just as easily

might surface: car keys, caulking gun,

whale rib the size of a park bench.

Boys rode their boats like bulls. Were bucked

and washed ashore with half the throttle fast beneath

the foam white knuckles of their fists.

Salt hitched my hair and scraped my skin.

Bottles in the cooler clinked like dice.

Nights I would wait for the first worm

to swallow the hook. The trick, I learned,

was not to force it, was to let the worm feel the pain

that comes from blindness and mistake.

Matthew Poindexter

Nostalgia

Last night when we were watching *Lassie*,
I remember thinking, isn't it a shame
that dogs don't bark like they used to?
When Mom and Dad were kids
the dogs were always barking, and usually
that meant a person in the township
had fallen down a well. Those were the days.
Isn't it a shame, how no one falls down a well anymore?
I say we take a Saturday to head out on the town
with our crowbars and pry some covers
off; shrug off their concrete tops. Give everyone a handle
of Evan Williams whiskey, smack them on the ass
and shout: *Have at it!* Then sit and wait
for the concerned collies to come running.
But no, if you want a good old-fashioned crisis,
the wholesome kind, you have to go way back—
before they added color to the picture,
before Nader came along and ruined all the fun.
Non-exploding cars! Paint without lead! Go way back,
or to some other world, like Australia.
And even there the women scream, *A dingo ate my baby!*

a lot less frequent than before,
which is kind of like their version of barking.
Here, it's all just, woof woof—you smell
like you could get me some bacon,
or, woof woof—I just took a dump
and if you don't pick it up immediately,
the city's going to fine you.
These days, I feel like I'm the one that's stuck
down in the well, and all that I can do
is tread water. Everything has the same harmlessness.
In the end, the well of blandeur is so deep
that I can't even tell if the dogs are barking or not.
They don't make barking like they used to.

Patrick Whitfill

Of Your Misguided Saints

> *Et t'aime d'autant plus, belle, que tu me fuis*
> —Baudelaire

Once your manager at Dairy Queen
caught you sneaking Schnapps into the Blizzard
machine again, he fired your seventeen-
year-old bony ass right then. Undeterred
and unemployed, you crammed inside your El
Camino all the Boone's and Patsy Cline
cassettes that you could find, and while "I Fall
to Pieces" filled the cab like a hymn at the shrine
of your misguided saints, you hung a kiss
past Carolina, promising you'd write.
Eventually, our town forgot your exodus,
as towns will do, but I still think of the night
before you left, the two of us, my Chevy.
How soft our bodies are, and slow. How heavy.

Kate Sweeney

Death of the Hired Hand, Hiawatha, Kansas

I loved his hands pulling that rattlesnake from the baler,
how the thing twitched slightly, as if shuddering in its sleep.

He fetched the shovel to grind off its head, that sick miracle
of jaw still opening and closing on the rusty spade.

I brought the body to grandmother who husked it and shaved off
the tender white kernels of tissue, curing enough meat

to feed one man. Its dried rattle is still a warning,
urging my memory to stay in the barn so I would not be the one

to find him writhing at the gate, gasping in a bloody-backed t-shirt,
while the bull in crimson-tipped horns looked on indifferently.

Acknowledgments

Carolyn Creedon's "Pied Beauty" previously published by *MARGIE*.

James Crew's "Sex in the Rain" previously published by *basalt*.

Alex Dimitrov's "White Fire" previously published by *Diode*.

Caitlin Doyle's "Thirteen" previously published by *Unsplendid*.

Warren Heiti's "From *The Uncollected Works of Sallie Chisum*" previously published by *Event*.

Adam Giannelli's "What We Know" previously published by *Smartish Pace*.

Jules Gibbs's "Pronghorn" previously published by *Spoon River Poetry Review*.

Pilar Gómez-Ibáñez's "Losing Bedrock Farm" previously published by *Indiana Review*.

Rae Gouirand's "January" previously published by *American Poetry Review*.

Michael J. Grabell's "Definition of Terms" previously published by *The Southwest Review*.

Rebecca Keith's "Epistolary" previously published by *Saint Ann's Review*.

Trey Moody's "Climate Reply" previously published by *American Letters & Commentary*.

Joshua Robbins's "The Man in Hopper's *Office in a Small City*" previously published by *Fourteen Hills*.

Stephanie Rogers's "On the Occasion of Her Annual Disappointment" previously published by *The Southern Review*.

Gretchen Steele Pratt's "Road Rising Into Deep Grass" previously published by *The Boston Review*.

Kate Sweeney's "Death of the Hired Hand, Hiawatha, Kansas" previously published by *RATTLE*.

Joe Wilkins's "Notes from the Journey Westward" previously published by *Beloit Poetry Journal*.

Johnathon Williams's "Dirge" previously published by *Pebble Lake Review*.

Contributors' Notes

AMANDA CHIADO is a graduate of California College of the Arts. Her poetry is forthcoming or appears in *Fence, Beeswax, The Dirty Napkin, The Rambler, Cranky,* and *Line 4*. She lives with her husband Fabio and daughter Isabella in San Jose, California, where she works as a California Poet in the Schools. She is finishing her first novel, and her most recent poems come from her working poetry manuscript, titled *Monsters, Heroes and Bimbos*.

BRANDON COURTNEY spent four years in the United States Navy. He is currently pursuing a BA in creative writing from Drake University in Des Moines, Iowa, where he is finishing his manuscript titled *When the Ocean Is an Autoclave*. This is his first notable publication.

JAMISON CRABTREE holds an MFA from the University of Arizona. His poems have appeared in *LIT, 42opus, poemeleon,* and *Verse Daily*.

After getting kicked out of college the first time around, CAROLYN CREEDON went to San Francisco and worked as a waitress, dancer, etc., for thirteen years. Since then she has graduated from Smith College and Washington University. She currently studies and lives in Charlottesville with her partner and her little black dog.

JAMES CREWS holds an MFA in poetry writing from the University of Wisconsin-Madison. His work appears or is forthcoming in *Prairie Schooner, Columbia, Best New Poets 2006,* and other journals. A chapbook, *Small Yellow Envelopes,* based on the life and work of artist Felix Gonzalez-Torres, is due out this year from Parallel Press, and another chapbook, *Bending the Knot,* recently won the Gertrude Press Poetry Award.

LAURA DAVENPORT is an MFA candidate at Virginia Commonwealth University in Richmond, Virginia. Her work has appeared or is forthcoming in *Breakwater Review, Boxcar Poetry Review,* and the *Helen Burns Poetry Anthology.*

KELLY DAVIO currently serves as poetry and reviews editor at *The Los Angeles Review* and reads for *Fifth Wednesday Journal.* Her recent and forthcoming publications include *Beeswax, Weave, Bellingham Review,* and *Gargoyle,* among others. She holds an MFA in poetry from Northwest Institute of Literary Arts, and makes her home in Seattle, Washington.

Poems by SALLY DAWIDOFF have appeared in diverse periodicals including *Ploughshares, BOMB,* and *American Journal of Nursing.* She has been an NEA fellow and was an Artist in Residence at Headlands Center in 2009. She teaches poetry workshops in New York.

DANIELLE CADENA DEULEN is currently a PhD student in English at the University of Utah. During 2007–2008, she was a Jay C. and Ruth Halls Poetry Fellow through the Wisconsin Institute for Creative Writing at the University of Wisconsin, Madison. She is a graduate of George Mason University's MFA Program in Poetry, the recipient of two Dorothy Sargent Rosenberg Poetry prizes, and a former fellow at the Virginia Center for the Creative Arts. Her work has appeared in journals such as *The Southern Review, The Indiana Review, Hayden's Ferry, Crab Orchard,* and others.

CHIARA DI LELLO is a double major in French Studies and Muslim Studies at Wesleyan University in Connecticut. In 2008 she was named a Connecticut Student Poet and toured as part of the Connecticut Poetry Circuit. She just returned from a semester in Morocco, where she studied French, Arabic, and history and spent quality time with the local stork and cat population. She was born in New York City.

KATY DIDDEN is pursuing her PhD in Literature and Creative Writing at the University of Missouri. She has poems published or forthcoming in journals such as *Crazyhorse, Hayden's Ferry Review, The Journal, Smartish Pace, Shenandoah,* and *Poetry.*

ALEX DIMITROV is the recipient of a Roy W. Cowden Fellowship from the Hopwood Awards at the University of Michigan. His poems and reviews have appeared in *The Southwest Review, Poets & Writers, Crab Orchard Review, Gargoyle,* and *The Portland Review,* among others. He is the founder of Wilde Boys, a queer poetry salon in New York City. More of his poems appear at alexdimitrov.blogspot.com.

A native of Manasquan, New Jersey, BEN DOMBROSKI recently received an MFA from Virginia Commonwealth University.

CAITLIN DOYLE spent 2008–2009 as the Writer-in-Residence at St. Albans School. Caitlin earned her MFA from Boston University, where she was the George Starbuck Fellow in Poetry. She received the Thomas Wolfe Scholarship in Creative Writing at UNC Chapel Hill, and has been awarded fellowships from the Virginia Center for the Creative Arts, the Vermont Studio Center, the Edward F. Albee Foundation, and others. Caitlin has received prizes through *The Atlantic,* the Academy of American Poets, and the Dorothy Sargent Rosenberg Foundation. Her publications include *The Warwick Review, The Boston Review, Measure, Rattle, The Louisville Review, Hanging Loose Magazine, Calyx,* and others.

CAITLIN DUBE lives in New York City. She holds a BA in English and American Literature and Language from Harvard, and an MFA from Columbia University. Her poems have appeared in *The Western Humanities Review.*

BARBARA DUFFEY is a Vice-Presidential Fellow in the PhD Program in Literature and Creative Writing at the University of Utah. Her poems have appeared or are forthcoming in *Indiana Review, American Letters & Commentary, Asimov's Science Fiction,* and *Prairie Schooner.* A *summa cum laude* graduate of the University of Southern California, she has worked as a telephone operator, an SAT math tutor, a paralegal, a volunteer on an archeological dig, a reading instructor for preschoolers to adults, and an instructor for Writers in the Schools. She coordinates the Agha Shahid Ali Prize at the University of Utah Press and lives in Salt Lake City with her husband, one dog, and two cats.

ADAM GIANNELLI is a graduate of the MFA program at the University of Virginia, where he was a Henry Hoyns Fellow. He is also the editor of *High Lonesome: On the Poetry of Charles Wright* (Oberlin College Press, 2006). His poetry has appeared in the *American Literary Review, Smartish Pace,* and *Phoebe.*

JULES GIBBS has been a recipient of a writing fellowship from the Ucross Foundation, and has twice won prizes for poetry from the Dorothy Sargent Rosenberg Foundation. Current poems appear or are forthcoming in *The Antioch Review, Salt Hill Journal, Stone Canoe, Born Magazine, MARGIE, Barrow Street, The Comstock Review, The New Anonymous, Broken Plate, The Alembic, Spoon River Poetry Review,* and elsewhere. In 2008, she moved to Syracuse, New York, and has been teaching at the Downtown Writers' Center, Syracuse, and to children in city schools. She will be in Houston, Texas, in the fall of 2009, teaching poetry at Inprint Houston, Inc., and working on her first manuscript.

PILAR GÓMEZ-IBÁÑEZ grew up in Wisconsin and earned an MFA in 2006 from Cornell University, where she was a Javits Fellow and taught writing for three years. She has received an AWP Intro Award, a Dorothy Sargent Rosenberg Prize, the Indiana Review Poetry Prize, and support from the Jentel Artist Residency Program and the Money for Women/Barbara Deming Memorial Fund. Her work has appeared in *Indiana Review, The Madison Review, Puerto del Sol,* and other journals. In 2007–2008 she was a writing fellow at the Fine Arts Work Center in Provincetown, Massachusetts.

RAE GOUIRAND's poems have appeared most recently in *American Poetry Review, jubilat, Bellingham Review, Forklift, Ohio, Columbia, MAKE Magazine, Tarpaulin Sky,* and *Bateau.* The winner of the Meijer Fellowship, the Hopwood Award, awards from the Academy of American Poets, and recent fellowships from the Vermont Studio Center and the Santa Fe Art Institute, she also received an award in 2009 from the Dorothy Sargent Rosenberg Foundation for outstanding work by emerging poets. She lives in Davis, California.

MICHAEL J. GRABELL's poems are forthcoming in *Best American Poetry 2009* and have been published in *Southwest Review, Columbia Poetry Review, Rattle, Sow's Ear Poetry Review, Inkwell, Borderlands,* and the *Tulane Review.* He is originally from New Jersey and studied creative writing at Princeton University. Last year, he moved from Dallas to New York, where he works at ProPublica, a journalism nonprofit dedicated to investigative reporting, and also mentors students in the MFA program at Western Connecticut State University.

WARREN HEITI is a PhD student and sessional instructor in philosophy at Dalhousie University in Halifax, Nova Scotia, Canada. His poems and reviews have been published in literary journals across Canada, and some of his work was anthologized in *Breathing Fire 2: Canada's New Poets* (Nightwood Editions, 2004).

SARA ELIZABETH JOHNSON holds an MFA in Creative Writing from the University of Oregon and a BA in English from Cornell University. Her poems have appeared or are forthcoming in *New England Review, Shenandoah, Willow Springs, Cutthroat, Iron Horse Literary Review,* and *Tampa Review.* She is the recipient of an AWP Intro Journals Project Award and a 2009–2010 Winter Fellowship from the Fine Arts Work Center in Provincetown. She was also a 2009 finalist for the Ruth Lilly Poetry Fellowship.

REBECCA KEITH holds an MFA in poetry from Sarah Lawrence College. She has received honors from *Atlantic Monthly* and *BOMB* magazine, was a finalist for the 2008 Laurel Review/GreenTower Press Midwest Chapbook Series Award and has twice been a poetry finalist for the Salem College Center for Women Writers International Literary Awards. Her poems and essays have appeared most recently in *The Laurel Review, Storyscape Journal,* and *The Millions,* and she is a founder and curator of the Mixer Reading Series in New York City.

SALLY ROSEN KINDRED is author of *Garnet Lanterns,* winner of the Anabiosis Press Chapbook Contest. She received a 2007 Individual Artist Fellowship in Poetry from the Maryland State Arts Council. Her poems have appeared or are forthcoming in *Poetry Northwest, Potomac Review, Spoon River Poetry Review,* and *Blackbird.*

BRIAN LEARY is the managing editor of 42opus.com. He lives in Brooklyn.

KEITH LEONARD is an MFA candidate at Indiana University. His poems have appeared or are forthcoming in *Quarterly West, Sentence, Georgetown Review, Naugatuck River Review,* and *Red Mountain Review.*

JENNIFER MOLNAR is author of the chapbook *Occam's Razor* (Main Street Rag Press). She is a graduate of George Mason University's MFA program in poetry, and her work has appeared or is forthcoming in *The Ledge, Salt Hill, Phoebe,* and elsewhere.

TREY MOODY lives with his wife in Lincoln, Nebraska, where he is pursuing a PhD in poetry at the University of Nebraska. His poems have appeared in *American Letters & Commentary, CutBank, Denver Quarterly, DIAGRAM, Quarterly West, Third Coast,* and elsewhere.

AMANDA PRITCHARD MOORE received her MFA in 2001 from Cornell University, where she studied beekeeping and bookmaking along with poetry. Since that time, she has mastered the art of the road trip, risotto, and growing up. She is a teacher at Cranbrook, an architectural and artistic paradise just outside of Detroit, where she lives with her husband and daughter.

MEGAN MORIARTY is an MFA candidate at Virginia Tech. Her poetry has appeared in *Opium Magazine, elimae,* and *At-Large Magazine.*

LAUREN MOSELEY received her MFA from the University of North Carolina at Greensboro, where she also served as poetry editor of *The Greensboro Review.* Her poems appear in recent issues of *The Southeast Review* and *Cimarron Review.* She currently teaches introductory English classes at UNCG and Guilford College.

CHRIS PERKOWSKI's poems have appeared in *Natural Bridge, Phoebe, Pleiades,* and *Cimarron Review.*

MATTHEW POINDEXTER is an undergraduate at the University of North Carolina.

GRETCHEN STEELE PRATT's poems have previously appeared or are forthcoming in *The Southern Review, The Iowa Review, Boston Review, Witness, Gettysburg Review, The Southwest Review, Indiana Review, AGNI Online, Witness, Jacket,* and on Poetry Daily. She currently teaches English at Wingate University and University of North Carolina at Charlotte.

After attending Princeton University, ROGER REEVES completed his BA in English at Morehouse College in 2003, graduating *magna cum laude*. He received an MA in English with a certificate in women's studies from Texas A&M University. His awards include the 2008 Ruth Lilly Fellowship from the Poetry Foundation, a Bread Loaf Work-Study Scholarship, two Cave Canem fellowships and an Alberta H. Walker Scholarship to the Provincetown Fine Arts Center. His poems have appeared or are forthcoming in *American Literary Review, Gulf Coast, Indiana Review, Poetry, Sou'wester,* and *Verse Daily*. He is an MFA candidate at the University of Texas James Michener Center.

JOSHUA ROBBINS holds an MFA from the University of Oregon and is a PhD candidate in English at the University of Tennessee, where he teaches poetry writing. His poetry was awarded the 2008 James Wright Poetry Award and has recently appeared or is forthcoming in *Third Coast, Mid-American Review, Hayden's Ferry Review, Fourteen Hills, New South, Southern Poetry Review, Copper Nickel,* and elsewhere.

STEPHANIE ROGERS grew up in Middletown, Ohio, and now lives in Brooklyn, New York. In 2007, she received her MFA in poetry from the University of North Carolina at Greensboro. She is a Pushcart Prize nominee, a two-time nominee for the Ruth Lilly Poetry Fellowship, and her poem "Symphony for Red" appeared in *Best New Poets 2006*. Her work has also appeared in *Another Chicago Magazine, The Southern Review, Pleiades,* and *Cream City Review,* among others. In 2008, she and Amber Leab co-founded the feminist film review Web site Bitch Flicks.

KATIE SCHMID is a first-year student in the University of Wyoming's Creative Writing MFA program. She is also the poetry associate editor for *The Dirty Napkin*, an online literary journal.

ARNOLD SEONG earned an MFA from the University of Washington in 2007. He lives and works in Seattle, and is finishing a manuscript titled *The Anatomy of Speech*. "Transplantation" is his first publication anywhere apart from his parents' refrigerator.

DAVID SILVERSTEIN is a NYC-area based artist. He has been awarded an Academy of American Poets prize, a Deus Loci White Mice prize, and has been published in several journals, including *The Amherst Review*, The New School's *LIT*, and *Pank*. More of his work appears at AnotherPointlessProduction.com.

MELISSA STEIN's poems have appeared in *The Southern Review, American Poetry Review, New England Review, Indiana Review, Gulf Coast, North American Review, Cimarron Review, National Poetry Review*, and many other journals and anthologies. Her work has won the Spoon River Poetry Review Editor's Prize Contest and the Literal Latté Poetry Awards, among others, and she has received residency fellowships from Yaddo, MacDowell, Djerassi, Montalvo, Ragdale, and the Virginia Center for the Creative Arts. She holds an MA in creative writing from the University of California at Davis, and works as a freelance writer and editor in San Francisco.

KATE SWEENEY holds an MFA in poetry from the University of Florida. Her chapbook, *Better Accidents*, was winner of the 2009 YellowJacket Press Chapbook Contest. Her work has appeared or is forthcoming in *Poetry East, Meridian, RATTLE, Spoon River*, and *Tampa Review*.

MICHAEL VERSCHELDEN was born into and raised by a pack of lawyers in Kansas. He has never attempted to hop boxcars, though he believes he has the agility. His poems have accused him of collusion and reckless abandonment, surfacing in *The Midwest Quarterly, The Kansas City Star, The Rockhurst Review*, and *Touchstone*. He appeared in 2007 at Bucknell University's Seminar for Younger Poets and in 2009 at the New York

State Summer Writers Institute in Saratoga Springs. He will join George Mason University's MFA program in fall 2009.

ERIC WEINSTEIN's poems have appeared in a variety of online and print publications, been nominated for inclusion in the annual Pushcart Prize anthology, and won several awards, including the Anne Flexner Award in poetry. He currently serves as poetry editor at *Prick of the Spindle* (www.prickofthespindle.com). A native of Nashua, New Hampshire, he currently lives in Hoboken, New Jersey.

Born and raised in Fresno, California, TANA JEAN WELCH currently exists among the oak trees and palmetto bugs of Tallahassee, where she's working toward a PhD in literature at Florida State. Her poems have recently appeared in *Beloit Poetry Journal, North American Review,* and *The Southern Review.*

After finishing his PhD from Texas Tech University, PATRICK WHITFILL spent a year in South Carolina as the writer-in-resident at HUBBUB. He currently serves as an adjunct at Wofford College. His poetry can be found in *West Branch, Mid-American Review, Iron Horse Literary Review, Poet Lore,* and *The Evansville Review,* among others.

JOE WILKINS was born and raised north of the Bull Mountains of eastern Montana. He now teaches writing at Waldorf College in Forest City, Iowa, and his recent work appears in *The Georgia Review, The Southern Review, Mid-American Review, Many Mountains Moving,* and *Orion.*

JOHNATHON WILLIAMS attends the MFA Program in Creative Writing at the University of Arkansas. When he isn't working as a freelance writer and Web developer, he produces and edits Linebreak.org, a weekly magazine of original poetry.

ANDY YOUNG is the co-editor of *Meena Magazine,* a bilingual Arabic-English literary journal, and teaches Creative Writing at New Orleans Center for Creative Arts. Her work has recently appeared in *Third Coast, Paste, Boulevard, Cincinnati Review,* and

Callaloo, as well as in journals in Lebanon, Egypt, Ireland, and Mexico. Her writing has also been included in the anthologies *We Begin Here* (Interlink Books, 2007) and *Voices of the Storm* (McSweeney's, 2006).

Participating Writing Programs

MFA Program in Creative Writing
American University
Department of Literature
4400 Massachusetts Avenue N.W.
Washington, DC 20016

Creative Writing Program
Arizona State
English Department
Tempe, AZ 85287

Master of Arts in Creative Writing
Boston University
236 Bay State Road
Boston, MA 02215
www.bu.edu/writing

Middlebury College
The Bread Loaf Writers' Conference
Kirk Alumni Center
Middlebury, VT 05753
www.middlebury.edu

MFA Program in Creative Writing
Brooklyn College
Department of English
2900 Bedford Avenue
Brooklyn, NY 11210

Program in Literary Arts
Brown University
Box 1923
Providence, RI 02912
www.brown.edu/Departments/Literary_Arts

Creative Writing Program
Colorado State University
Department of English
359 Eddy Building
Fort Collins, CO 80523-1773

MFA in Creative Writing
Columbia College Chicago
English Department
600 S. Michigan Avenue
Chicago, IL 60605
www.colum.edu/MFApoetry

School of the Arts
Columbia University Writing Division
Dodge Hall
2960 Broadway, Room 400
New York, NY 10027-6902

Creative Writing Program
Inland Northwest Center for Writers
501 N Riverpoint Blvd., Suite 425
Spokane, WA 99202
www.ewuMFA.com

MFA in Creative Writing
Emerson College
120 Boylston Street
Boston, MA 02116-1596

Writing Fellowship
Fine Arts Work Center in Provincetown
24 Pearl Street
Provincetown, MA 02657
www.fawc.org

MFA Program in Creative Writing
Florida International University
Department of English, Biscayne Bay Camp
3000 N.E. 151st Street
North Miami, FL 33181

Department of English
Florida State University
Williams Building
Tallahassee, FL 32306-1580
english.fsu.edu/crw

Creative Writing Program
George Mason University
4400 University Drive
MS 3E4
Fairfax, VA 22030
creativewriting.gmu.edu

MFA in Creative Writing
Goddard College
123 Pitkin Road
Plainfield, VT 05667
www.goddard.edu

Creative Writing Program
Hollins University
P.O. Box 9677
Creative Writing Program
Roanoke, VA 24020

MFA Program
Hunter College
68th and Lexington
New York, NY 10065

The Writing Seminars
Johns Hopkins University
135 Gilman Hall
3400 North Charles Street
Baltimore, MD 21218-2690

Writing Program
Kalamazoo College
English Department
1200 Academy Street
Kalamazoo, MI 49006
www.kzoo.edu/programs/?id=12&type=1

Creative Writing Program
Kansas State University
Department of English
108 ECS Building
Manhattan, KS 66506
www.ksu.edu/english/programs/cw.html

Asian American Poetry Retreat
Kundiman
245 Eight Avenue, #151
New York, NY 10011

Mentor Series Program
The Loft Literary Center
Suite 200, Open Book
1011 Washington Avenue
South Minneapolis, MN 55414-1246
www.loft.org

English Department
Louisiana State University
260 Allen
Baton Rouge, LA 70803
english.lsu.edu/dept/programs/creative_writing

Program in Creative Writing
McNeese State University
P.O. Box 92655
Lake Charles, LA 70609
www.MFA.mcneese.edu

Creative Writing Program
Minnesota State University, Mankato
230 Armstrong Hall
Mankato, MN 56001
www.english.mnsu.edu

Department of English
New Mexico State University
Box 30001
Department 3E
Las Cruces, NM 88003-8001
www.nmsu.edu

Graduate Writing Program
The New School
66 West 12th Street, Room 505
New York, NY 10011

Graduate Program in Creative Writing
New York University
58 W. 10th Street
New York, NY 10011

Creative Writing Program
Oberlin College
Peters G31
Oberlin, OH 44074
www.oberlin.edu/crwrite

Creative Writing Program
Ohio State University
Department of English, 421 Denney Hall
164 West 17th Avenue
Columbus, OH 43210-1370

MFA Creative Writing Program
Old Dominion University
5th floor, Batten Arts and Letters Building
Hampton Boulevard
Norfolk, VA 23529
www.luisaigloria.com

Master of Fine Arts in Creative Writing
Pacific University
2403 College Way
Forest Grove, OR 97116
www.pacificu.edu/as/MFA

MFA in Creative Writing
Pennsylvania State University
Department of English
S. 144 Burrowes Building
University Park, PA 16802

MFA Program
San Diego State University
Department of English and
    Comparative Literature
5500 Campanile Drive
San Diego, CA 92182-8140

Office of Graduate Studies
Sarah Lawrence College
1 Mead Way
Bronxville, NY 10708-5999

MA in English, Creative Writing
Southeastern Missouri State
MS 2650, English Department
Cape Girardeau, MO 63701

Program in Creative Writing
Syracuse University
Department of English
401 Hall of Languages
Syracuse, NY 13244-1170

Creative Writing Program
Texas A&M University
Deptartment of English
Blocker 227 - TAMU 4227
College Station, TX 77843-4227

MFA Program in Creative Writing
Texas State University
Department of English
601 University Drive, Flowers Hall
San Marcos, TX 78666
www.txstate.edu

Creative Writing Program
Texas Tech University
English Department
Lubbock, TX 79409-3091
www.english.ttu.edu/cw

Program in Creative Writing
University of Alabama
Department of English
P.O. Box 870244
Tuscaloosa, AL 35487-0244
www.as.ua.edu/english/08_cw

Fairbanks Program in Creative Writing
University of Alaska
Department of English
P.O. Box 755720
Fairbanks, AK 99775-5720
www.uaf.edu/english

Creative Writing Program
University of Arizona
Department of English
Modern Languages Building #67
Tucson, AZ 85721-0067
cwp.web.arizona.edu

Program in Creative Writing
University of Arkansas
Department of English
333 Kimpel Hall
Fayetteville, AR 72701
www.uark.edu/depts/english/PCWT.html

Graduate Creative Writing Program
University of California, Davis
Department of English
Davis, CA 95616

Creative Writing Program
University of Denver
Department of English
2140 South Race Street
Denver, CO 80208
www.du.edu/english/gradcwr.html

MFA@FLA
University of Florida
Department of English
P.O. Box 11730
Gainesville, FL 32611-7310
www.english.ufl.edu/crw

Creative Writing Program
University of Hawaii
English Department
1733 Donaghho Road
Honolulu, HI 96822
www.english.hawaii.edu/cw

Creative Writing Program
University of Houston
Department of English
R. Cullen 229
Houston, TX 77204-3015

Creative Writing Program
University of Idaho
Department of English
Moscow, ID 83843-1102
www.class.uidaho.edu/english/CW/
    MFAprogram.html

Program in Creative Writing
University of Iowa
102 Dey House
507 North Clinton Street
Iowa City, IA 52242

Creative Writing Concentration
University of Louisiana at Lafayette
Department of English
P.O. Box 44691
Lafayette, LA 70504-4691
www.louisiana.edu/Academic/LiberalArts/
    ENGL/Creative.html

Creative Writing Program
University of Maryland
Department of English
3119F Susquehanna Hall
College Park, MD 20742
www.english.umd.edu/programs/CreateWriting

MFA Program for Poets and Writers
University of Massachusetts
452 Bartlett Hall
130 Hicks Way
Amherst, MA 01003-9269
www.umass.edu/english/eng/MFA

MFA Program in Creative Writing
University of Minnesota
Department of English
207 Church Street S.E.
Minneapolis, MN 55455
english.cla.umn.edu/creativewriting/
    program.html

Program in Creative Writing
University of Missouri-Columbia
Department of English
107 Tate Hall
Columbia, MO 65211
www.missouri.edu/~cwp

Master of Fine Arts in
    Creative Writing Program
University of Missouri-St. Louis
Department of English
8001 Natural Bridge Road
St. Louis, MO 63121
www.umsl.edu/~mfa/

Department of English
University of North Texas
1155 Union Circle #311307
Denton, TX 76203-5017
www.engl.unt.edu/grad/grad_creative.htm

Creative Writing Program
University of Notre Dame
356 O'Shaughnessy Hall
Notre Dame, IN 46556-0368
www.nd.edu/~alcwp/

MFA in Writing Program
University of San Francisco
Program Office, Lone Mountain 340
2130 Fulton Street
San Francisco, CA 94117-1080

MFA Program
University of South Carolina
Department of English
Columbia, SC 29208

The Center for Writers
The University of Southern Mississippi
118 College Drive #5144
Hattiesburg, MS 39406
www.centerforwriters.com

Michener Center for Writers
University of Texas
J. Frank Dobie House
702 East Dean Keeton Street
Austin, TX 78705
www.utexas.edu/academic/mcw

Creative Writing Program
University of Texas at Austin
1 University Station B5000
English Department
Austin, TX 78712

Creative Writing Program
University of Utah
255 South Central Campus Drive
Room 3500
Salt Lake City, UT 84112

Creative Writing Program
University of Virginia
Department of English
P.O. Box 400121
Charlottesville, VA 22904-4121
www.engl.virginia.edu/creativewriting

Creative Writing Program
University of Washington
Box 354330
Seattle, WA 98195-4330

MFA in Creative Writing
University of Wisconsin-Madison
Department of English
600 N. Park Street
Madison, WI 53706
www.creativewriting.wisc.edu

Creative Writing Program
University of Wisconsin-Milwaukee
Department of English
Box 413
Milwaukee, WI 53201

Creative Writing Program
University of Wyoming
Department of English
P.O. Box 3353
Laramie, WY 82071-2000
www.uwyo.edu/creativewriting

Unterberg Poetry Center/Writing Program
92nd Street Y
1395 Lexington Avenue
New York, NY 10128
www.92Y.org/poetry

Master of Fine Arts in Writing
Vermont College
36 College Street
Montpelier, VT 05602
www.tui.edu

MFA in Creative Writing Program
Virginia Commonwealth University
Department of English
P.O. Box 842005
Richmond, VA 23284-2005

MFA Program
Virginia Tech
English Department
Blacksburg, VA 24061
www.english.vt.edu/graduate/MFA

MFA Program for Writers
Warren Wilson College
P.O. Box 9000
Asheville, NC 28815-9000

Weslyan University
Wesleyan Writers Conference
294 High Street, Room 207
Middletown, CT 06459
www.wesleyan.edu/writers

Creative Writing Program
West Virginia University
Department of English
P.O. Box 6296
Morgantown, WV 26506-6269
www.as.wvu.edu/english

MFA in Professional Writing
Western Connecticut State University
181 White Street
Danbury, CT 06470
www.wcsu.edu/writing/MFA

Graduate Program in Creative Writing
Western Michigan University
Department of English
6th Floor Sprau
Kalamazoo, MI 49008-5092

Whidbey Writers Workshop
P.O. Box 639
Freeland, WA 98249
www.writeonwhidbey.org/MFA

Canada

Sage Hill Writing Experience
Box 1731
Saskatoon, SK S7K 3S1
www.sagehillwriting.ca

Creative Writing Program
University of British Columbia
Buchanan E462-1866 Main Mall
Vancouver, BC V6T 1Z1
www.creativewriting.ubc.ca

Creative Writing Research Group
University of Calgary
Creative Writing, c/o English Department
University of Calgary
Calgary, AB T2N 1N4
www.english.ucalgary.ca/cw

Bachelor of Fine Arts
University of Victoria
Department of Writing
P.O. Box 1700, STN CSC
Victoria, BC V8W 2Y2

Participating Magazines

32 Poems Magazine
P.O. Box 5824
Hyattsville, MD 20782
www.32poems.com

AGNI
Boston University
236 Bay State Road
Boston, MA 02215
www.bu.edu/agni

Alligator Juniper
Prescott College
220 Grove Avenue
Prescott, AZ 86301
www.prescott.edu/highlights/alligator_juniper

Anti-
4347 Osceola Street
St. Louis, MO 63116
anti-poetry.com

The Antioch Review
Antioch University
P.O. Box 148
Yellow Springs, OH 45387
www.review.antioch.edu

Bat City Review
The University of Texas at Austin
Department of English
1 University Station B5000
Austin, TX 78712
www.batcityreview.com

Bellevue Literary Review
NYU School of Medicine
Department of Medicine
550 First Avenue, OBV-A612
New York, NY 10016
www.BLReview.org

Beloit Poetry Journal
P.O. Box 151
Farmington, ME 04938
www.bpj.org

The Bitter Oleander Press
4983 Tall Oaks Drive
Fayetteville, NY 13066-9776
www.bitteroleander.com

Black Warrior Review
University of Alabama
Box 862936
Tuscaloosa, AL 35486
bwr.ua.edu

Blackbird
Virginia Commonwealth University
Department of English
P.O. Box 843082
Richmond, VA 23284-3082
www.blackbird.vcu.edu

Blood Orange Review
1495 Evergreen Ave NE
Salem, OR 97301
www.bloodorangereview.com

Boston Review
35 Medford Street
Suite 302
Somerville, MA 02143
bostonreview.net

Boxcar Poetry Review
401 S. La Fayette Park Pl. #309
Los Angeles, CA 90057
www.boxcarpoetry.com

Cave Wall
P.O. Box 29546
Greensboro, NC 27429-9546
www.cavewallpress.com

Coconut
2331 Eastway Road
Decatur, GA 30033
www.coconutpoetry.org

Colorado Review
Colorado State University
The Center for Literary Publishing
9105 Campus Delivery / Dept. of English
Fort Collins, CO 80523-9105
coloradoreview.colostate.edu

Contrary
3133 S. Emerald Avenue
Chicago, IL 60616
www.contrarymagazine.com

The Cream City Review
University of Milwaukee-Wisconsin
Department of English
P.O. Box 413
Milwaukee, WI 53201
www.uwm.edu/Dept/English/ccr

Dappled Things
2876 S. Abingdon Street, C-2
Arlington, VA 22206
www.dappledthings.org

The Dead Mule
Second Street
Washington, NC 27889
helenl.wordpress.com

FIELD
Oberlin College Press
50 North Professor Street
Oberlin, OH 44074
www.oberlin.edu/ocpress

Florida Review
University of Central Florida
English Department
P.O. Box 161400
Orlando, FL 32816-1400
www.flreview.com

The Georgia Review
University of Georgia
285 S. Jackson Street
Athens, GA 30602-9009
www.thegeorgiareview.com

Gertrude
P.O. Box 83948
Portland, OR 97283
www.gertrudepress.org

The Gettysburg Review
Gettysburg College
300 N. Washington Street
Gettysburg, PA 17325-1491
www.gettysburgreview.com

Gold Wake Press
5 Barry Street
Randolph, MA 02368
goldwakepress.org

The Greensboro Review
University of North Carolina, Greensboro
MFA Writing Program
3302 Moore Humanities and Research
Greensboro, NC 27402-6170
www.greensbororeview.org

Guernica
557 W. 149th Street, #19
New York, NY 10031
guernicamag.com

Gulf Coast
University of Houston
Department of English
Houston, TX 77204-3013
www.gulfcoastmag.org

Harvard Review
Harvard University
Lamont Library
Cambridge, MA 02138
hcl.harvard.edu/harvardreview

Hayden's Ferry Review
Arizona State University
The Virginia G. Piper Center
    For Creative Writing
P.O. Box 875002
Tempe, AZ 85287-5002
www.haydensferryreview.org

The Hudson Review
684 Park Avenue
New York, NY 10065
www.hudsonreview.com

IMAGE
3307 Third Avenue West
Seattle, WA 98119
www.imagejournal.org

In Posse Review
4128 Mississippi St # 4
San Diego, CA 92104
webdelsol.com/InPosse

Indiana Review
Indiana University
Ballantine Hall 465
1020 E. Kirkwood Avenue
Bloomington, IN 47405-7103
www.indianareview.org

The Iowa Review
University of Iowa
308 EPB
Iowa City, IA 52242-1408

The Journal
The Ohio State University
Department of English
164 W. 17th Avenue
Columbus, OH 43210
www.english.osu.edu/journals/thejournal

Juked
110 Westridge Drive
Tallahassee, FL 32304
www.juked.com

The Kenyon Review
Kenyon College
Finn House
102 W Wiggin Street
Gambier, OH 43022-9623
www.kenyonreview.org

Ledge Magazine
40 Maple Avenue
Bellport, NY 11713
www.theledgemagazine.com

Literary Bird Journal
Dept of English/098
University of Nevada, Reno
Reno, NV 89557
www.literarybirdjournal.org

The Los Angeles Review
Red Hen Press
P.O. Box 3537
Granada Hills, CA 91394

The Massachusetts Review
University of Massachusetts
South College
Amherst, MA 01003
www.massreview.org

Memorious: A Journal of New Verse and Fiction
3424 Brookline Avenue, Apt 16
Cincinnati, OH 45220
www.memorious.org

Michigan Quarterly Review
University of Michigan
0576 Rackham Building
915 East Washington Street
Ann Arbor, MI 48019-1070
www.umich.edu/~mqr

Mid-American Review
Bowling Green State University
Department of English
Box W
Bowling Green, OH 43403
www.bgsu.edu/midamericanreview

The Minnetonka Review
P.O. Box 386
Spring Park, MN 55384

Mississippi Review
The University of Southern Mississippi
Box 5144
Hattiesburg, MS 39406-0001
www.mississippireview.com

The Missouri Review
University of Missouri
357 McReynolds Hall
Columbia, MO 65211

The National Poetry Review
P.O. Box 2080
Aptos, CA 95001-2080
www.nationalpoetryreview.com

New Letters
University of Missouri-Kansas City
5101 Rockhill Road
Kansas City, MO 64110
www.newletters.org

Nimrod
The University of Tulsa
800 S. Tucker Dr.
Tulsa, OK 74104-3189
www.utulsa.edu/nimrod

Ninth Letter
234 English, Univ. of Illinois
608 S. Wright Street
Urbana, IL 61801
www.ninthletter.com

No Tell Motel
c/o Reb Livingston
11436 Fairway Drive
Reston, VA 20190
www.notellmotel.org

Orion
187 Main Street
Great Barrington, MA 01230
www.orionmagazine.org

Phoebe
George Mason University
4400 University Drive
MSN 2C5
Fairfax, VA 22030-4444
phoebejournal.com

Pleiades
The University of Central Missouri
Department of English and Philosophy
Martin 336
Warrensburg, MO 64093
www.ucmo.edu/englphil/pleiades

Ploughshares
Emerson College
120 Boylston Street
Boston, MA 02116
www.pshares.org

Poemeleon: A Journal of Poetry
Riverside, CA 92506
www.poemeleon.org

Prairie Schooner
University of Nebraska-Lincoln
201 Andrews Hall
P.O. Box 880334
Lincoln, NE 68501-9988
prairieschooner.unl.edu

Raving Dove
P.O. Box 28
West Linn, OR 97068
www.ravingdove.org

River Styx
Big River Association
3547 Olive Street Suite 107
Saint Louis, MO 63103
www.riverstyx.org

Salamander
Attn: Jennifer Barber
Suffolk University English Department
41 Temple Street
Boston, MA 02114
www.salamandermag.org

Sentence
Firewheel Editions
Box 7
181 White Street
Danbury, CT 06810
www.firewheel-editions.org

Shenandoah
Washington and Lee University
Mattingly House
2 Lee Avenue
Lexington, VA 24450-0303
shenandoah.wlu.edu

Silenced Press
449 Vermont Place
Columbus, OH 43201
silencedpress.com

Smartish Pace
P.O. Box 22161
Baltimore, MD 21203
www.smartishpace.com

The Southeast Review
Florida State University
English Department
Tallahassee, FL 32306
www.southeastreview.org

The Southern Review
Louisiana State University
Old President's House
Baton Rouge, LA 70803
www.lsu.edu/thesouthernreview

The Southwest Review
Southern Methodist University
307 Fondren Library West
P.O. Box 750374
Dallas, TX 75275-0374
www.smu.edu/southwestreview

St. Petersburg Review
Box 2888
Concord, NH 03301
www.stpetersburgreview.com

Stirring : A Literary Collection
218 Stevens Dr
Hattiesburg, MS 39401
www.sundress.net/stirring

Subtropics
English Dept. P.O. Box 112075
University of Florida
Gainesville, FL 32611
www.english.ufl.edu/subtropics

The Tusculum Review
Tusculum College
60 Shiloh RD
P.O. Box 5113
Greeneville, TN 37743
www.tusculum.edu/tusculumreview

Third Coast
Western Michigan University
Department of English
Kalamazoo, MI 49008-5092

Unsplendid
c/o Douglas Basford
169 Mariner Street, Apt. 2
Buffalo, NY 14201
www.unsplendid.com

upstreet
Ledgetop Publishing
P.O. Box 105
205 Summit Road
Richmond, MA 01254-0105
www.upstreet-mag.org

Verse
University of Georgia
Department of English
Athens, GA 30602
www.versemag.blogspot.com

Washington Square
New York University
Creative Writing Program
58 W. 10th Street
New York, NY 10011
www.washingtonsquarereview.com

The Yale Review
Yale University
P.O. Box 208243
New Haven, CT 06520-8243

Yellow Medicine Review
Southwest Minnesota State University
11 Florence Avenue
Binghamton, NY 13905
www.yellowmedicinereview.com/id13.html

ZYZZYVA
P.O. Box 590069
San Francisco, CA 94159-0069
www.zyzzyva.org

Canada

Apple Valley Review:
  A Journal of Contemporary Literature
c/o Queen's Postal Outlet
Box 12
Kingston, ON K7L 3R9
www.applevalleyreview.com

Event
Douglas College
Box 2503
New Wesminster, BC V3L 5B2
event.douglas.bc.ca